Survey of the New Testament

as taught by
Dr. Bill Mounce

BiblicalTraining.org
Because Your Spiritual Growth Matters

Survey of the New Testament
Copyright © Student's Guide Copyrighted 2020 BiblicalTraining.org. All Rights Reserved. Course content and outline Copyrighted 2020 Dr. Bill Mounce. All Rights Reserved.

Requests for information should be addressed to:

BiblicalTraining.org
523 NE Everett St
Camas WA 98607

ISBN: 9781074055066

All Scripture quotations, unless otherwise indicated, are taken from the Holy Bible, New International Version®, NIV®. Copyright ©1973, 1978, 1984, 2011 by Biblica, Inc.™ Used by permission of Zondervan. All rights reserved worldwide. www.zondervan.com The "NIV" and "New International Version" are trademarks registered in the United States Patent and Trademark Office by Biblica, Inc.™

All rights reserved. No part of this publication may be reproduced, stored in a retrieval system, or transmitted in any form or by any means—electronic, mechanical, photocopy, recording, or any other—except for brief quotations in printed reviews, without the prior permission of BiblicalTraining.org.

Printed in the United States of America

https://www.biblicaltraining.org/survey-new-testament/bill-mounce

Table of Contents

Overview v
Your Speaker vi
Weekly schedule vii
Facilitator's Guide viii
BiblicalTraining.org x
1. Class Introduction 1
2. How was the Bible Written? 5
3. Can We Trust Our Bible? 14
4. How We Received Our Bible 21
5. Mark 1-5 30
6. Mark 6-11 38
7. Mark 11-13 46
8. Mark 14-16 55
9. Matthew 1:1-5:12 66
10. Matthew 5:17-7:29; 28:19-20 77
11. Luke 87
12. John 1-12 96
13. John 13-21 105
14. Acts 1-12 113
15. Acts 13-15 and Galatians 123
16. Acts 15:36-18:22 and 1-2 Thessalonians . . . 133
17. Acts 18:23-21:26 and 1 Corinthians 1-6 . . . 145
18. 1 Corinthians 7-16 and 2 Corinthians 155
19. Romans 1-4 164

20.	Romans 5-11	174
21.	Romans 9-16	185
22.	Acts 21:27-28:31 and Ephesians	194
23.	Philippians	205
24.	Colossians and Philemon	216
25.	The Pastoral Epistles	228
26.	Hebrews	239
27.	James	251
28.	Peter and Jude	262
29.	John's Letters	274
30.	Revelation	283
	Statement of Faith	294

Overview

Title: Survey of the New Testament

Speaker: Dr. Bill Mounce

GOALS

1. To understand the basic structure of the New Testament, its core themes and players
2. To be challenged to draw your basic theology from the biblical text
3. To learn how to apply theology to life in gracious and God-honoring ways

REQUIREMENTS

1. 40 sessions
2. Three hours per week (lesson and discussion)

PREREQUISITES

None

FORMAT

Audio

Lesson

Your Speaker

Dr. Bill Mounce lives as a writer in Washougal, Washington. He is the President of BiblicalTraining.org, a non-profit organization offering world-class educational resources for discipleship in the local church. He also runs BillMounce.com, a site committed to helping people learn biblical Greek..

Formerly Bill was a preaching pastor at a church in Washington state, and prior to that a professor of New Testament and director of the Greek Program at Gordon-Conwell Theological Seminary. He also taught at Azusa Pacific University for ten years.

Bill is the author of the bestselling Greek textbook, Basics of Biblical Greek, and many other resources. He was the New Testament chair of the English Standard Version translation of the Bible, and is currently serving on the NIV translation committee.

Robin and Bill have been married since 1983 and have three children.

EDUCATION

Ph.D. 1981, in New Testament. Aberdeen University, Aberdeen, Scotland.

M.A. 1977, in Biblical Studies. Fuller Theological Seminary, Pasadena, California.

B.A. 1975, in Biblical Studies, minor in Greek. Bethel College, St. Paul, Minnesota; Western Kentucky University, Bowling Green, Kentucky, 1971-74.

Weekly schedule

Listen or watch the lesson. The lesson for each chapter is designed to be listened to outside of your meeting. Each lesson lasts for an hour. This is a crucial step. If the meeting time with your fellow students is going to be productive and encouraging, everyone in the group needs to have listened to and wrestled with the lesson.

Take notes. This guide has the outline for each lesson with a summary of the teaching for each major point. If you are unable to take notes while listening to the lesson, please work through the guide at some point before your meeting.

Questions. Each chapter closes with a series of questions. Some of the questions are data based, confirming that you understand the information. Other questions are more reflective, helping you move beyond the important accumulation of knowledge to challenging you to think through what you are learning about God, yourself and others, and finally to application. Our encouragement is to think through your answers before your meeting and then use the meeting to share your thoughts and interact with others.

Meeting. Meet together with your group.

MEETING TOGETHER

While some people may have to study on their own, we strongly recommend finding a group with which you can study.

A group provides encouragement to finish the class.

Interacting with others, their understanding and insight, is the most effective way to sharpen your own thoughts and beliefs.

Just as you will need the help of others from time to time, so also they will need your help.

Facilitator's Guide

If you are facilitating the group or mentoring an individual, here are some suggestions that should help you.

Your role is to facilitate. This is not an opportunity for you to teach. In fact, the less visible role you take, the better. Your role is to listen and bring out the best in the other people.

Preparation. Be sure to have done your homework thoroughly. Have listened to the lesson and think carefully through the questions. Have an answer for each question that will get the conversation going. A great question is, "What is the Lord teaching you this week?"

Creativity. What works to help one person understand may not help another. So listen to the conversation and pray that the Lord help you bring out the greatest interaction among all the people.

Correct error. This is difficult. If someone says something that isn't right, you don't want to come down on them, telling them they are wrong and shutting down their participation. On the other hand, if you let an obvious error pass, the rest of the group may think you agree and what was said was correct. So look for gracious ways to suggest that perhaps the person's comment was incorrect.

Focus. Stay focused on Jesus and the Bible, not on church or religious traditions.

Lead the discussion. People don't want to listen to a sharing of common ignorance. Lead by asking questions that will prompt others to think.

Silence. Don't be afraid of silence. It may mean nothing more than people are thinking. But if the conversation lags, then ask thought-provoking questions to get the discussion started, and then step out of the way.

Discipleship. Be acutely aware of how you can mentor the people in the group. Meet with them for coffee. Share some life with them. Jesus' Great Commission is to teach people to obey, and the only way this happens is in relationship.

Different Perspectives. People process information and express themselves in different ways based on their background, previous experience, culture, religion and other factors. Encourage an atmosphere that allows people to share honestly and respectfully.

Privacy. All discussions are private, not to be shared outside the group unless otherwise specified.

Goal. The goal of this study is not just increased knowledge; it is transformation. Don't be content with people getting the "right" answers. The Pharisees got the "right" answer, and many of them never made it to heaven (Matt 5:20).

Relationships. Share everyone's name, email and phone number so people can communicate during the week and follow up on prayer requests. You may want to set up a way to share throughout the week using Slack or WhatsApp.

Finish well. Encourage the people to make the necessary commitment to do the work, think reflectively over the questions, and complete the class.

Prayer. Begin and end every meeting with prayer. Please don't do the quick "one-prayer-covers-all" approach. Manage the time so all of you can pray over what you have learned and with what you have been challenged. Pray regularly for each individual in the meeting.

BiblicalTraining.org

BiblicalTraining.org is not-for-profit ministry that gives all people access to a world-class Christian education at no cost. Our classes range from new believers to biblical literacy ("Foundations"), deeper Bible study ("Academy"), and seminary-level training ("Institute").

We are a 501(c)3 not-for-profit and rely solely on the donations of our users. All donations are tax deductible according to the current US tax codes.

DISTINCTIVES

World class. All Bible classes are taught by world-class professors from major seminaries.

Holistic. We want to see students move through content to deep reflection and application.

Configurable. Ministries can use BT lectures as well as their own to design their educational program.

Accessible. BiblicalTraining is a web-based ministry whose content is provided at no cost.

Community-based. We encourage people to learn together, in mentor/apprentice relationships.

Broadly evangelical. Our materials are broadly evangelical, governed by our Statement of Faith, and are not tied to any one church, denomination or tradition.

Partners. We provide the content and delivery mechanisms, and our partner organizations provide the community and mentoring.

1

Class Introduction

Lesson 1: Introduction

I. **WHAT IS THE PURPOSE OF THIS CLASS?**

   Train people so they will know what the bible teaches and that they will be transformed

II. **WHO IS THIS CLASS FOR?**

   New Christians, people with a desire to learn about the faith and leaders

III. THREE STAGES:

A. Head

What the bible teaches - *Info about the Bible*

B. Heart

Theology so you learn more about who God is and his relationship to you - *theology - use the Statement of Faith is used as the grid*
Processing the info

C. Hands
Training for
Transformation so you change how you live your life

Spiritual

Ultimate goal is transformation.
Apply it
The purpose of the time is to grow us as christians

IV. GENERAL CLASS INFORMATION

Questions

1. Why are you in this class? What would you like to gain? What motivates you?

2. What have you done previously to learn what the Bible teaches?

3. How do you apply what the bible teaches to your life so that it changes who you are and makes a difference in how you act toward others.

4. What's one recent example of how your faith made a difference in how you acted toward someone?

2

How was the Bible Written?

I. PASSING ON INFORMATION DURING JESUS'S LIFE

Most teaching was oral and their culture valued transferring information by memory

II. PERIOD OF ORAL TRANSMISSION

The early church was preserving the stories about the life of Jesus and beginning to formulate an understanding of what it meant.

III. WAS THE EARLY CHURCH ACCURATE? (JESUS SEMINAR)

The early church had eyewitnesses, the Holy Spirit reminded them of what Jesus said, and the early Christians were willing to die for what they believed.

Lesson 2. How was the Bible Written?

IV. PERIOD OF WRITING: AUTHORSHIP AND AUTHORITY

Mark was written by the 50's CE and the other New Testament documents within the next few decades. The authors were mostly apostles or people closely associated with the apostles.

V. WRITING OF THE SYNOPTICS

A. "Synoptic Problem"

How do you explain the similarities and differences that exist among the gospels of Matthew, Mark and Luke? See Matthew 3:7-10 and Luke 3:7-9; Matthew 27:44 and Luke 23:39-43.

B. What do the Gospels say about themselves?

The goal of the gospel writers was to record events in the life of Jesus to show you who Jesus is and what he taught during his time on earth. See Luke 1:1-4, John 20:30-31 and John 21:25.

[handwritten: How to make it orderly. Try to make a point.]

STANDERED

C. Reconstruction

WRITTEN TO JEWS — TO GENTILES

Mark was written first, then Matthew and Luke who used Mark and a document referred to as "Q" for their sources.

D. Harmonization *(STORIES DIFFERENT BUT COMPHRABLES)*

The stories in each of the gospels can be true even though there are some differences in the way the accounts are recorded.

E. The Importance of Trusting the Bible *IS FUNDAMENTAL TO YOUR LIFE.*

You must decide whether or not you trust the Bible and consider the Bible authoritative for the way you live your life.

VI. INSPIRATION

A. Definition

The source of Scripture is God.

B. Infallibility

Scripture is true in all that it affirms.

C. Inerrancy

There are no internal contradictions in Scripture and no contradictions between Scripture and science and history.

2 Peter 1:20 *(handwritten)*

D. The Method of Inspiration

mystery (handwritten)

The dynamic view of inspiration asserts that Scripture is the very words of God, but that God did not override the writing styles and personalities of the writers.

E. The Scope of Inspiration

The view of plenary inspiration asserts that you can trust the accuracy of the Bible there is a reasonable explanation for each apparent contradiction.

Questions

1. This lesson has dealt with trusting the Bible from many different angles. What from this lesson brings you the most confidence that the testimony of Scripture is accurate?

2. What hesitations or questions do you still have about the truthfulness of Scripture? Or, what are the primary objections you hear from others around you?

3. Which theory of inspiration ("inspiring," dictation, or dynamic) do you find most convincing, and why?

4. If you were entrusted in an important piece of information and were not able to write it down, how would you go about ensuring that you remembered it properly?

5. Someone who is not a Christian will most likely not believe that the Holy Spirit helped the apostles remember the words and works of Jesus with accuracy. How could you explain this belief to them in a way that they can see it makes sense to you? Think mostly about how to present this rationally, and not emotionally or purely as an issue of faith.

6. Explain the "Synoptic problem" in your own words.

7. Role play a scenario in which one person thinks the gospel was intentionally or accidentally changed during the time of oral transmission and the other does not.

8. Role play a situation in which someone says you can't trust the gospels because they were copied, and therefore cannot be trusted.

9. Do the same again but this time dealing with the charge that they are so different that they cannot be trusted.

10. Discuss some ideas you have about talking to others about the Bible who have differing presuppositions than your own (e.g., miracles are impossible, so these

11. What are some ideas you have in talking to others about the Bible who have differing presuppositions than your own (e.g., miracles are impossible, so these passages in the Bible must be false)?

3

Can We Trust Our Bible?

I. **THE SCOPE OF INSPIRATION**

   A. **"Limited" Inspiration (Infallibility)**

   1. **Definition**

      Scripture is true in statements that relate to faith and practice, but not necessarily in other areas.

   2. **Problems**

      It's difficult to determine how to categorize each statement in Scripture, this position is contrary to 2 Timothy 3:16, the New Testament asserts the historical veracity of Old Testament facts and events and if the authors of Scripture couldn't record historical facts accurately, how do we know that they got anything else right?

B. Plenary Inspiration (inerrancy)

1. Definition

Scripture has no errors

2. Arguments for Inerrancy

Scripture claims to be inerrant and truth is an essential element of God's character,

Solutions to Apparent Contradictions

The secular source could be wrong, people who witness the same event often describe the details differently so there may be a scenario where both versions could be true (harmonization), you may be misinterpreting the text of Scripture.

II. WHAT DOES INSPIRATION NOT MEAN?

Inspiration applies to the original documents, not copies, inspiration does not apply to footnotes, titles, headings, verse numbers, punctuation, grammatical errors, figures of speech, or approximations, translations are not inspired.

III. WHY DO I THINK THE BIBLE IS INSPIRED?

The Bible claims that it is from God, it makes sense to believe that it is inspired, the work of the Holy Spirit in my life, it is historically accurate, it is internally consistent, numerous prophecies that were made have been fulfilled.

Questions

1. Do you believe the Bible is inspired? Why or why not?

2. What is the most convincing argument for you of the truthfulness of the Scriptures?

3. What do you think the role of the Holy Spirit is in belief in the truthfulness of Scripture?

4. Take some time to reflect on whether you live as if you believe Scripture is inspired. Are there places in your life or heart that God is speaking to through his word?

5. When you think about how Scripture is God speaking, and how it is truthful just as he is—how do these ideas affect how you live? How does God want these doctrines to affect your life?

6. Explain the difference between limited inspiration and plenary inspiration.

7. Recall the parts of the text that are not inspired (i.e., not part of the original autograph, e.g., chapter and verse numbers). What implication does this have, if any, on how you read Scripture?

8. Identify and discuss some of your peers' or culture's main objections to the truthfulness of Scripture.

9. Choose one of the most significant main objections identified in #3 above, and discuss how you might address that objection.

10. Role play a situation in which someone believes that the Gospels are full of contradictions. Explain how we might understand some of these differences.

4

How We Received Our Bible

I. INTRODUCTION

It's helpful to understand how the Bible was written and came to us in its current form.

II. CANONIZATION

A. Why the Canon Developed

The apostles were beginning to die, Christians were beginning to be persecuted for their faith, there was a rise of heresy and people creating false writings.

B. Terms

Canon means the collection of books that are from God and should be in the Bible.

C. Three Criteria for Canonicity

Apostolic authorship, harmony of doctrine and tone, continual usage in the church as a whole.

D. Is the Canon Closed?

Arguments regarding whether or not the Canon should be considered closed.

E. Why I Think the Church Got it Right

No other writings meet the criteria and at the core, it's an issue of faith.

III. TRANSMISSION OF THE WRITINGS

There are differences in the manuscripts because they were copied by hand over hundreds of years.

IV. TEXTUAL CRITICISM

Textual criticism is the process of studying the differences in manuscripts to determine what the original document was.

We have over 5,000 Greek manuscripts, 99 percent of the text is sure, the 1 percent where there are some differences do not affect a core biblical doctrine.

V. TRANSLATIONS

A. Difficulties

The New Testament was written in ancient Greek, languages express thoughts differently, words have a range of meaning, contemporary languages are changing.

B. The Word "Literal"

It is impossible to translate directly from one language to another.

C. Translation Philosophy

1. Formal Equivalence

The translation is word for word as much as possible.

2. Dynamic Equivalence

The goal is to translate the meaning even if the grammatical form is different.

3. Paraphrase

Paraphrase is a thought for thought translation

4. Running Commentary

Versions where the author describes in their own words what it means to them.

VI. CONCLUSIONS

Trust your Bible to be an accurate translation, read more than one translation when you study

Questions

1. Do you believe the canon is closed or not? Why? How does Jude 3 affect this discussion?

2. Do you think the church was right in their decision of the canon? Can you think of any situations in which the issue of the canon has caused someone to stumble in their faith?

3. Does it bother you to know that there are differences among the manuscripts? Why do you think God allowed this to happen?

4. In light of all of the different manuscripts and translations of the Bible, do I trust the one I hold in my hand? Why?

5. Do you have a personal preference for how "formal" or "dynamic" your Bible translation is? What version do you prefer to read, and why?

6. What kind of things could have happened without authority in the church?

7. Review the three criteria of inclusion in the canon. Do you understand each one? If someone wanted to include a new book in the canon that is part of the New Testament Apocrypha, how would you respond?

8. What are the three points made about our current situation with manuscripts? How would you answer someone you claimed that central theological doctrines were brought into question due to manuscript differences?

9. Do you have any stories of embarrassing moments when someone translated word-for-word from one modern language into another? How might these stories help you show someone else the problems of translating the Bible?

10. What is "formal equivalence" and what is an example of that type of translation philosophy? Some of these types of translations claim to be "non-interpretive." How would you respond?

11. What is "dynamic equivalence" and what is an example of that type of translation philosophy? Can you think of any verses where the translator's theology or interpretation of meaning was added to the Bible? Is this the right thing to do?

5

Mark 1-5

I. **INTRODUCTION**

   Gospel of Mark by Bill Lane, New International Commentary on the New Testament, Gospel of Mark by David Garland, NIV Application Commentary

II. **GEOGRAPHICAL STRUCTURE AND PRIMARY CHARACTERISTICS**

   Beginnings, ministry in Galilee, travel ministry, Jerusalem ministry

III. **JOHN THE BAPTIST**

   This was an exciting time because John the Baptist was getting people ready for the coming of the Messiah and the new covenant.

IV. JOHN BAPTIZES JESUS

Jesus chose this as a way to formally begin his public ministry

A. "Beloved Son"

This is a quotation from Psalm two that was used to address the king on his day of coronation.

B. "Suffering Servant"

This is a quote from Isaiah 42:1 referring to the coming Messiah.

V. THE KINGDOM OF GOD (MARK 1:14-15)

Jesus redefined the Kingdom of God as a spiritual reality that was present because of his coming to earth and also something that will come in its fullness in the future.

VI. TWO DAYS IN THE LIFE OF JESUS (MARK 1:16-3:6)

Mark chooses to include stories about Jesus to show you who he is.

VII. "SON OF MAN" (MARK 2:1-12)

A title that Jesus used to refer to himself that has roots in the Old Testament. It indicates both humility and servanthood as well as exaltation and power.

VIII. PARABLES

The primary way that Jesus used to teach people about the kingdom of God.

A. Definition

Stories taken from everyday life for the purpose of teaching one main point.

B. Details

A parable has one main point and the details are secondary.

C. Three Rules for Interpreting Parables

A parable has one main point, the details are secondary in importance to the main point and the parable must have made sense in Jesus' day.

D. Summary of Jesus's Parables

The theme of most of the parables of Jesus is the Kingdom of God.

IX. MIRACLE STORIES (MARK 4:35-5:43)

Jesus was more than just a good man, he was God in the flesh.

Questions

1. The Jews of Jesus's day thought of the Christ as an earthly ruler. Before we are too quick to judge them, do we do the same today? Are there ways in which we think of greatness in material and not spiritual terms?

2. Jesus was God's Servant; his mission was not to be served but to serve. Do you think that you and your church fully understand this concept? How does it manifest itself? How does Mark 9:35 work itself out in your individual and corporate life?

3. In what ways has the church thought of the kingdom of God and its own mission in earthly terms? What are the ramifications of understanding God's kingdom in spiritual terms?

4. The dual nature of God's kingship and his kingdom can be a difficult concept to comprehend. Talk about it in your group and make sure you understand it. How does the Promise/Fulfillment nature of reality affect you on a daily basis? What struggles do you have because of it? What victories do you likewise have?

5. What examples today illustrate the truth of Jesus's two "days" of acceptance and rejection? Why is it that religious leaders often have the most struggle with the truth?

6. What are the four basic divisions of Jesus's life, and what characterized the second and third segments?

7. In what ways do you see Jesus as an Ezekiel-type Son of Man?

8. In what ways do you see Jesus as a Danielic Son of Man?

9. In what ways do you see them combined?

10. Parables can be tricky to understand without a commentary giving you the necessary background. But spend some time looking at parables and try to ascertain the main point of each. Be patient; you may have lots of differing opinions on this one.

11. If someone told you that Jesus was just a good man, how would you use the stories of Mark 4 and 5 to show them that they are wrong? This is a good thing to practice out loud with people.

6

Mark 6-11

I. SECOND MAJOR PHASE OF JESUS'S LIFE (MARK 8:27-11:11)

The second part of Mark's Gospel describes the travel ministry of Jesus.

A. Peter's Confession as the Hinge

Peter's confession that Jesus is the Messiah is the culmination of the account of Jesus' Galilean ministry and the beginning of the account of his travel ministry.

B. Three Cycles

Jesus predicts his death, there is a misunderstanding of what discipleship is and then Jesus teaches about discipleship.

1. Unit 1: Mark 8:31-9:29

   Discipleship is total because Jesus expects his disciples to be fully devoted, it is essential for your salvation and it is life long.

2. Unit 2: Mark 9:30-10:31

3. Unit 3: Mark 10:32-11:11

II. HEART AND HAND ISSUES

   A. Sanctification

   B. Perseverance and Assurance

   C. Presenting the Gospel

Questions

1. In an overall sense, how do you feel about the statement that discipleship is "total, essential, and lifelong"? (This is not a question asking for theological discussion, but your personal response).

2. How do you feel about the word "Lordship"? Are you going to use it, or have past abuses made it too difficult to use?

3. Do you believe that discipleship is a matter of life and death? Is it optional or mandatory? Why?

4. How might you be tempted to "save" your life? What does it look like, practically, to lose your life for Christ? Stay away from philosophical ideas; be concrete.

5. How will you express your belief that no one can snatch you out of the Father's hand, and yet that you must work out your salvation?

6. How do feel about what we have called "event Christianity"? (The idea of one event, like praying a prayer, guaranteeing salvation). Have you ever heard it taught? Have you ever seen it lived out? Have you ever seen it practiced outside the United States?

7. In your own words, what does it mean to "deny" yourself?

8. In your own words, what does it mean to "take up your cross"?

9. What does a life of denial look like? Please be concrete and specific? What does it not look like?

10. Christians talk a lot about be servants; have you ever seen some truly be a servant to others? What does it look like, and what does it not look like? How have you been a servant to someone this week?

11. Can you think of any modern parallels to the metaphor of "ransom"?

12. Do role playing on the question of carnality. One person should insist that they are going to get to heaven, even if they have ongoing sin in their life, and that how they lives out their life will have no affect on their eternal destiny.

13. This is really important. Prepare the two-minute presentation of the gospel that is sufficiently complete that if a person responds they will in fact go to heaven. What might a person add that would be unnecessary?

7

Mark 11-13

I. CURSING THE FIG TREE

Jesus uses the fig tree as a metaphor for Israel because they haven't produced spiritual fruit.

II. CONFLICT STORIES

When the Pharisees try to entrap Jesus with questions, he answers them using parables.

III. MARK 13: THE OLIVET DISCOURSE

Jesus taught the crowds on the Mount of Olives.

A. Apocalyptic Literature

This is a genre of literature in the first century that uses images to describe events that will happen in the end times when God intervenes in history.

B. The Destruction of the Temple, the Return of Jesus, and the End (Mark 13:1-8)

Jesus describes the order of events.

C. Persecution and the Ethics of Eschatology (Mark 13:9-13)

Jesus describes persecution his disciples will face and also tells that that, "the one who endures to the end will be saved."

D. The "Abomination of Desolation" (Mark 13:14-20)

This was likely a reference to the coming destruction of the temple in Jerusalem in 70 ad.

E. False Christs (Mark 13:21-23)

Miracles by themselves do not produce authenticity.

F. Signs of the Coming of the Son of Man (Mark 13:24-27)

When Christ returns, it will be globally visible, public and unmistakeable.

G. Parable of the Fig Tree (Mark 13:28-31)

These verses are most likely referring to the destruction of the temple in Jerusalem in ad 70.

H. Final Warnings (Mark 13:32-37)

Only God the Father knows the exact time that Jesus will return to earth.

I. Other Passages on Jesus's Return

1. **Acts 1:7-8**

   We don't know exactly when Jesus will return, but it's important for us to do what God has called us to do.

2. **Matthew 24:37-25:46**

   Always be ready for Jesus' return because you don't know exactly when it will be.

J. Prophecy

Old Testament prophets wrote specific descriptions of the coming of the Messiah hundreds of years before Christ came.

1. Typology or Double Fulfillment

God gave prophecies that are often fulfilled in similar ways in different times in history.

2. Foreshortening

Sometimes a prophet envisions something that looks to them like one event but is actually something that is extended over a long period of time.

IV. SUMMARY OF MARK 13

The temple will be destroyed. Jesus will return at the end of the age and there may not be a specific sign to warn you.

Questions

1. When you read apocalyptic literature, either that dispersed in the gospels, the book of Revelation, or the book of Daniel, how do you tend to read? Do you take the text literally, or more symbolically? How might what you've learned in this lesson about the apocalyptic genre change how you read?

2. Has this lesson changed what you previously thought about eschatology, or the end times? How so? In particular, how can you live in light of the idea that eschatology is ethical?

3. Eschatology is controversial and discussions often turn mean-spirited. Is there anything in your discussion of these questions that perhaps you wish now you could have stated another way? What if people who believe differently were present? Would you have changed the discussion? This is a significant question, since eschatology is ethical.

4. The final warnings in Mark 13 and the parables in Matthew 24-25 all teach the suddenness of Jesus's return and that we must be ready. What do you think of this? Does your life need to change at all in order to be ready?

5. Do you see persecution, wars, famine, or destruction around you? How does Jesus want you to respond, in light of Mark 13?

6. Identify the main characteristics of the apocalyptic genre.

7. How will you carefully respond if someone says that current wars and earthquakes are signs that the end of the earth is imminent?

8. What is the difference between typology and foreshortening?

Lesson 7. Mark 11-13

9. Can you summarize your eschatological beliefs? Summarize what will happen at the end of times.

10. Identify and answer the disciples' questions.

8

Mark 14-16

I. LAST NIGHT WITH DISCIPLES (MARK 14:1-52)

The Jewish leaders wanted to arrest Jesus and kill him secretly because he was popular with the people.

II. THE PASSOVER

Jesus celebrates the Passover with the disciples and show them how it symbolizes what he is about to do.

A. The Exodus as the Historical Background

The first Passover was the last of the ten plagues placed on Egypt. Putting the blood of a lamb around their door was a symbol that the Israelites belonged to God and it protected them.

B. Jesus Redefines Passover

Jesus says the Passover now points to God's greatest act of salvation, Jesus' death on the cross, in addition to being a reminder of how God saved his people from Egypt.

C. 1 Corinthians 11

An explanation of how the celebration of communion is a reinterpretation of the Passover which points to the death of Christ on the cross.

D. The New Covenant

Both Jeremiah and Ezekiel prophesied that god would establish a new covenant.

E. Three Views on the Lord's Supper

People have different views on the significance of the Lord's Supper, also referred to as communion.

1. Transubstantiation and Automatic Forgiveness

The Roman Catholic tradition is that the bread and wine in communion become the literal body and blood of Christ and when you take it, God's grace automatically goes to you and makes a spiritual change.

2. Consubstantiation

This is the view that Christ's body and blood was physically present, but the bread and wine weren't actually his body.

3. Symbolic View

Some people think that communion is a symbol of the death of Christ.

4. Response to Transubstantiation and Consubstantiation

Both views fail to acknowledge that Jesus is using a metaphor. Transubstantiation ignores the doctrine of sufficiency of Christ's sacrifice.

5. Response to the Symbolic View

What you eat and drink in communion represents Christ's death on the cross.

6. Past, Present, and Future Aspects of Communion

We look back at the death of Jesus, we are proclaiming what God has done and we look forward to the day that we will eat and drink with Jesus.

7. Terms and Frequency

Some traditions refer to communion as a sacrament, and some as an ordinance. Scripture does not mandate how often we should celebrate it.

III. THE FINAL EVENTS OF JESUS'S LIFE

The Gospel of Mark gives us quite a few details about the final days of the life of Jesus.

A. The Garden of Gethsemane

After Jesus had prayed, Judas betrayed him. He was put on trial, then scourged and crucified.

B. The Death of Jesus

Jesus' death on the cross and what he said in the process is significant prophetically and spiritually.

C. Atonement

The doctrine of what happened on the cross.

1. What the Atonement Is

Jesus took on the curse of the law in order to pay the penalty for the sin of you and everyone else throughout history.

2. Terms that Describe the Atonement

Sacrificial atonement, propitiation and redemption are words that describe atonement.

3. Debates over Atonement

Jesus' death satisfying God's anger against sin vs. an example of self-giving love that motivates us to love in the same way.

4. Heart Issues

God's love and his justice motivated him, sin is serious, what Jesus did on the cross is sufficient and the message of the Gospel is exclusive because only Jesus could do anything about it.

D. The Resurrection

Jesus was dead and came back to life in a physical body.

E. The Significance of Three Days

Jewish was that the spirit of a dead person would leave the body after three days.

F. **The Purpose and Implications of the Resurrection**

It was a public validation that Jesus' death accomplished what he said it would, it's the guarantee of our resurrection, it's an encouragement to his followers that his power is at work in us and it's an exhortation to us about how we should live our lives.

Questions

1. How is the new covenant different from the old covenant? How would your life be different if you lived in Old Testament times in terms of how you relate to God? Try to think of practical, concrete examples.

2. Do you emphasize one motivation for the atonement—love or justice—more than the other? Why do you think? Does anything need to change in your thinking?

3. Are there times in your life when you do not believe that Jesus's death on the cross was sufficient to forgive all your sin, or the sins of another? How does God want you to respond to this truth?

4. What are some concrete ways in which Jesus's resurrection impacts your life on a daily basis?

5. The implications of the resurrection are that it is a validation of all that Jesus said and accomplished, it guarantees our resurrection, it is meant to encourage us since the same Holy Spirit lives in us, and sin no longer has power over us. Are there any of these implications of the resurrection that God wants you to more fully live into? Be concrete as to how.

6. What do you think "this is my body" means? Do you think the Lord's Supper is a "sacrament" or an "ordinance"? Why? What would you do if you dropped the "elements"? Would you make croutons out of the bread?

7. How could we change the manner in which we take communion to reflect the three time frames of 1 Corinthians 11:26? What aspects of your current method of celebrating communion help you see its true significance?

8. Discuss how you would share the gospel in light of the atonement? Avoid using theological terms.

9. Role play someone saying that Jesus died merely as an example of self-giving love, how would you respond? What if they said that Jesus didn't have to die in order for us to get to heaven?

10. How would you counsel someone who said that they had sinned so grievously that they don't believe God could possibly forgive them?

9

Matthew 1:1-5:12

I. **THE BIRTH OF JESUS**

   A. The Genealogy

   Jesus is a descendant of King David

   B. The Angel's Announcement

   An angel tells Joseph that Mary is pregnant and still a virgin and the child will be the Messiah.

C. The Virgin Birth

1. Differing Positions on the Supernatural

Materialists or naturalists believe in a closed system of the material world in which no supernatural events can occur. Some people believe in an open system that believes there can be a cause outside of nature for events that happen.

2. The Importance of Believing in the Virgin Birth

The Bible says that miracles can happen, the Bible says that the birth of Jesus was a miracle and the Bible teaches that Jesus is God.

II. THE DOCTRINE OF THE INCARNATION

A. Definition

Jesus was both fully God and fully human. It's an essential element of the gospel and necessary in order for Jesus to make atonement for our sins.

B. Philippians 2

Jesus gave up the independent exercise of his divine power and lived by the power of the Spirit.

The Sermon on the Mount

I. RESOURCES

Sermon on the Mount by Carson, Christian Counterculture by John Stott, and some commentaries

II. INTERPRETING THE SERMON ON THE MOUNT

Jesus speaks in absolutes and the ethical requirements are high.

A. Already, but Not Yet

The Kingdom of God has come, but some aspects are yet to be fulfilled.

B. Avoid Oversimplification

> Give the teachings their full force but don't be simplistic when considering the imagery.

C. The Concern is the Heart

> Jesus wants your whole-hearted commitment.

III. INTRODUCTION TO THE BEATITUDES

The Beatitudes are the core, and the rest of the Sermon on the Mount explains what they mean.

A. Verse 3: Blessed are the Poor in Spirit

> You recognize your inability to be approved by God on your own.

B. Verse 4: Blessed are Those who Mourn

   You mourn before God because you recognize your spiritual bankruptcy.

C. Verse 5: Blessed are the Meek

   You don't assert yourself over others in pride and arrogance.

D. Verse 6: Blessed are those who Hunger and Thirst for Righteousness

   You pursue God as the source of righteousness.

E. Verse 7: Blessed are the Merciful

   As we realize our spiritual condition, we treat others with mercy.

F. Verse 8: Blessed are the Pure in Heart

In the deepest places in our heart, we must be fully devoted to God.

G. Verse 9: Blessed are the Peacemakers

If we are meek and merciful, we will seek peace.

H. Verses 10-12: Blessed are Those who are Persecuted for Righteousness's Sake

Rejoice and be glad when you are persecuted for your faith.

I. **Call to Action**

   1. **The Salt of the Earth**

      We should be living our lives in a way that is counter-cultural.

   2. **The Light of the World**

      We should live our lives in a way that brings attention to God to the people in our sphere of influence.

   3. **Wholehearted Commitment**

      The Beatitudes do not leave room for self-reliance or part-time Christianity.

Questions

1. Do you think believing in the virgin birth is important? Do you have any trouble believing in the virgin birth? Why?

2. Do you think the incarnation has a bearing on the doctrine of the atonement? If so, what?

3. It will perhaps take some time to come to grips with the difficulties in understanding the Sermon on the Mount. Most of us want it straight and simple. As we saw, this doesn't work in this passage. Talk together about the issues.

4. What does it mean to be "blessed"? How does this definition change your view or affect your life?

5. Have you ever mourned over your spiritual bankruptcy? What did it look like? What good came out of this difficult time?

6. How do you experience the reality that that the kingdom is here, but not yet in its fullness? Where do you see this in your life, and how do you think God wants you to respond?

7. Role play a discussion where one person believes in a closed system, and another in an open system. As one topic, talk about how each system explains the presence of good and evil.

8. Discuss how you would show someone that scientific approaches to reality are based on faith, and come up with an explanation for why a Christian view of reality is preferable.

9. Using your own words, explain the doctrine of the "incarnation."

10. Role play a situation where someone says they are a Christian but do not believe Jesus was fully human. Have the other person respond.

11. Explain the "already but not yet" approach to reading the Sermon.

12. A fun exercise is to paraphrase the Beatitudes. This means to say them in your own words, but bringing out their fuller meaning. Go ahead and try it

10

Matthew 5:17-7:29; 28:19-20

I. **INTRODUCTION TO THE SERMON ON THE MOUNT**

   A. **Undivided Loyalty: Righteousness (Matt. 5:17-48)**

   Go requires not only external obedience, but your heart.

   B. **Introduction (Matt. 5:17-20)**

   Jesus came to fulfill the Old Testament Law, not to abolish it.

C. Anger and Murder (Matt. 5:21-26)

If you are angry with someone, it's the same as murdering them.

D. Lust and Adultery (Matt. 5:27-30)

If you have lustful intent toward someone, it's the same as committing adultery.

E. Divorce (Matt. 5:31-32)

Divorce shouldn't happen except in cases of immorality.

F. Oaths (Matt. 5:33-37)

Keep your word.

G. Retaliation (Matt. 5:38-42)

Personal self-sacrifice displaces personal retaliation.

H. Hatred (Matt. 5:43-47)

Love and pray for your enemies.

I. Conclusion (Matt. 5:48)

Strive to have the same attitude and character as God and depend on him for the strength to do it.

II. **UNDIVIDED LOYALTY: ACTS OF PIETY (MATT. 6:1-18)**

- A. **Introduction (Matt. 6:1)**

- B. **Almsgiving (Matt. 6:2-4)**

    Give to the needy in secret, not to get attention.

- C. **Fasting (Matt. 6:16-18)**

    When you fast, don't let others know you are doing it.

- D. **Prayer (Matt. 6:5-15)**

    Pray sincerely and in private. Follow the model that Jesus gave us.

E. Undivided Loyalty: Total Commitment (Matt. 6:19-24)

F. Treasure (Matt. 6:19-21)

   Commit yourself totally to Jesus, not to material possessions.

G. Two Masters (Matt. 6:24)

   You can only serve one master.

H. Undivided Loyalty: Total Trust (Matt. 6:25-34)

   Don't worry. Seek God's Kingdom and he will provide everything you need.

Lesson 10. Matthew 5:17-7:29; 28:19-20

I. Final Instructions (Matt. 7:1-12)

   Check yourself out before you point out a problem in someone else.

J. Conclusion: Only Two Options (Matt. 7:13-27)

   You must choose the wide gate or the narrow gate.

III. THE GREAT COMMISSION (MATT. 28:18-20)

   As you go, make disciples, teaching them and baptizing them, and Jesus will be with you.

Questions

1. In the Sermon on the Mount, Jesus is speaking forcibly. Do you feel that it is impossible to meet Jesus's standards? If it feels impossible, what would encourage you to still try?

2. In the Sermon on the Mount, Jesus focuses a lot on the internal motivations of the heart, rather than just the external behaviors. Reflect on whether there are places in your life where you do things externally, but your heart is not involved. What can you do to change this?

3. Do you feel like you desire retaliation against anyone in your life? How can the Beatitudes and the Lord's prayer help you or someone else with this?

4. What general lessons have you learned through reading the Lord's Prayer? How will this prayer modify how you pray?

5. Many Christians try to deny the connection between treasures and the heart, but Jesus makes it clear that our treasures show the location of our hearts. Reflect on what the primary things you spend money on and what this says about your heart. Is there anything you can pray for God to change in your heart here?

6. From Matthew 28, reflect on how Jesus "being with you always" impacts your enacting of the Great Commission.

7. Make a list of when anger is right, and when it is wrong.

8. On the topic of lust, discuss the difference between temptation and sin.

9. Have one person represent each side in a discussion: Based on the Sermon on the Mount, is it okay to take a tax deduction on charitable gifts, or for a donor to have his name placed on a building she or he paid for?

10. Discuss whether you think that you should forgive someone even if they have not admitted their sin, have not repented, and have not asked for repentance. What are practical steps for doing this?

11. Discuss whether you believe prayer moves God to do what he might not otherwise do.

12. Consider whether there is someone in your life for whom God wants you to partner with him in "making disciples." What can you do?

11

Luke

I. INTRODUCTION TO LUKE

The author, Luke, was a Greek physician, writing primarily for a Greek audience. Luke made it clear that the gospel was for everyone, including women and the poor, which were two disenfranchised groups in his society.

II. BIRTH NARRATIVE

Luke emphasizes that even events surrounding the birth of Jesus were a reminder that the Gospel is for all people.

III. TEMPLE VISIT

Jesus began to realize as a young man that God was his father.

IV. BEGINNINGS OF MINISTRY AND TEMPTATION

Jesus began his public ministry when he was about 30 years old. After he was baptized, the Holy Spirit led him into the wilderness to be tempted for 40 days.

V. EARLY MINISTRY

A. Rejection in Nazareth

Jesus spoke in the synagogue in his home town and people rejected him.

B. Capernaum

Capernaum became the center of Jesus' ministry

C. Luke's Version of the Beatitudes

Possibly a way that Jesus began many of his sermons

VI. FOUR STORIES ABOUT "OTHERS"

These are stories about people who are outside the sphere of normal Jewish religious activity.

A. The Centurion's Servant

Jesus commends the centurion for his faith

B. The Widow's Son

Widows were considered at the bottom of the social ladder in that society.

C. The Sinful Woman

A sinful woman anoints the feet of Jesus while he is eating a meal with a group of Pharisees.

D. The Women Accompanying Jesus

A group of women was part of a larger group that followed Jesus.

VII. ADDITIONAL STORIES

A. The Parable of the Good Samaritan

A story Jesus told to answer the question, "Who is my neighbor?"

B. The Lord's Prayer

God wants us to pray to him boldly.

C. Woe Sayings

Jesus rebuked the religious hypocrites.

D. Stories that Define Discipleship

Radical Christianity requires a high cost and is often not peaceful.

E. God Seeks the Lost

Parables illustrating God's desire to seek and find the lost.

Questions

1. Reflect on whether there anyone or any group of people in your life whom you think are beyond God's reach. In light of the Gospel of Luke, how can you respond?

2. Who specifically in your life can you be a "good neighbor" to in the same way that the good Samaritan was?

3. Reflect on whether we judge those within normal religious circles to be "better" than those who are not.

4. How does the way Jesus involves and acts with women influence you personally?

5. Reflect on the radical call to discipleship in Luke 12-18. What impact do these have on your life?

6. Identify what groups tend to be the "socially outcast" in your own community. How are they typically treated?

7. How can your church or community more effectively reach out the disenfranchised?

8. Discuss what keeps people from being absolutely bold in coming to God and asking him for things in prayer.

9. Discuss what it means that Luke's "Sermon on the Mount" is different than Matthews. Is this bothersome? What are some solutions?

10. God's heart is to seek the lost, and there is great rejoicing when even one is found (Luke 15). Come up with an action plan for yourself or your church that mirrors the heart of God in this way.

12

John 1-12

I. **INTRODUCTORY ISSUES**

II. **CRITICAL ISSUES**

Accuracy of John's account, it is theologically more developed, Jesus moves from dialogue to monologue.

A. Date and Purpose of Writing

The Gospel of John was written in the late first century for the purpose of showing that Jesus is the Messiah.

B. Structural Overview

Prologue, book of signs, passion week, epilogue

III. PROLOGUE: THE DIVINE LOGOS (JOHN 1:1-18)

Jesus is God.

IV. THE BOOK OF SIGNS (JOHN 1:19-12:50)

Seven signs with the purpose of showing who Jesus is.

A. John the Baptist (John 1:19-34)

The forerunner of Jesus.

B. The Wedding at Cana and Cleansing the Temple (John 2)

Jesus turned water into wine at a wedding. When he went to the temple and saw that they had turned the court of the Gentiles into a marketplace, he overturned the tables and released animals to protest how irreligious they had become.

C. Nicodemus and the Necessity of Rebirth (John 3)

Jesus talks about being baptized in the water and the spirit and also believing in Jesus and having eternal life.

D. "Belief" in John

According to John, belief is not only intellectual assent, but transferring our trust out of ourselves and into Jesus.

E. The Samaritan Woman (John 4)

Jesus talks to the Samaritan woman about true worship.

F. Jesus Heals like his Father (John 5)

When Jesus referred to himself as Son of God, he was making himself equal with God.

G. Feeding the 5000 and the "I Am" Statements (John 6)

In John 10:30, Jesus said, "I and the Father are one." The Jews knew that Jesus was saying that he is God.

H. Continued Conflict with the Jews (John 7-8)

Jesus made statements about his deity that were related to symbolism in the Jewish festivals they were celebrating.

I. **The Man Born Blind (John 9)**

   Jesus heals a blind man but the religious leaders won't accept that he did it by the power of God.

J. **The Good Shepherd (John 10)**

   Jesus knows us and we know him.

K. **Raising Lazarus from the Dead (John 11)**

   Jesus demonstrates the he is the resurrection and the life.

L. **The Triumphal Entry and Rejection (John 12)**

   Jesus goes to Jerusalem a few days before the Passover celebration and the Jewish leaders and plotting a way to kill him.

Questions

1. What part of the prologue of John impacts you the most?

2. Does John's prologue convince you that Jesus is divine? Why or why not?

3. Like the man born blind (John 9), we all have testimonies and ways in which we can share our stories in powerful ways. Reflect on what God has done in your life and how you can share that with others.

4. Chapter 10 about the good shepherd is a chapter of marvelous encouragement. What from it encourages you the most?

5. Read chapter 11 on the raising of Lazarus. What does this chapter express about the character of God?

6. Practice explaining to someone who Jesus by walking them through from the prologue of John.

7. Identify the main issues people have with the authenticity of the Gospel of John. Talk about how you might address one of these

8. Identify the purpose of the Gospel of John, and where you see John doing this in a few places throughout his Gospel.

9. Explain why the "I am" statements were so offensive to the Jews.

10. Identify each of the seven signs in the John 1-12. Which seems most powerful and why?

13

John 13-21

I. STRUCTURAL OVERVIEW

II. THE UPPER ROOM DISCOURSE (JOHN 13-17)

    A. Servanthood (John 13:1-20)

        Jesus taught servanthood and modeled it with his life.

B. Foot Washing as an Ordinance?

It's not taught in the New Testament as an ordinance like baptism or communion, but it can be a valuable experience.

C. A New Commandment of Love (John 13:34-35)

Love one another as Christ has loved you.

A Definition of Love

In humility, count others as more significant than yourselves. (Philippians 2:3-4)

D. The Upper Room Discourse Continues (John 14)

Jesus reminds them that he is God and comforts and encourages them.

E. The Holy Spirit

1. Monotheistic and Trinitarian

God exists eternally in three persons – Father, Son, Holy Spirit—equal in essences and divine perfection.

2. Another Helper (John 14:15-17)

The Holy Spirit dwells in us to continue the ministry that Jesus began.

3. Brings All to Remembrance (John 14:25-26)

Jesus promised the disciples that the Holy Spirit would cause them to remember what he told them.

4. Bears Witness (John 15:26)

One of the functions of the Holy Spirit is to illuminate what Jesus did and what he taught.

5. Convicts (John 16:7-15)

The Holy Spirit convicts the world of its sin, its lack of righteousness and judgment.

6. Abide in Christ (John 15)

Jesus uses the image of a vine and branches to illustrate the idea of abiding in him.

F. High Priestly Prayer (John 17)

1. Jesus Prays for "Himself" (John 17:1-5)

Jesus wants to glorify God the Father.

2. **Jesus Prays for the Eleven Disciples (John 17:6-19)**

   Jesus prays for unity and to protect them from the evil one.

3. **Jesus Prays for Future Disciples (John 17:20-26)**

   Jesus prays that they would love each other and live in unity so people would know that God has sent him.

Questions

1. If you were one of the twelve, what thoughts would be going through your mind as Jesus draws closer to washing your feet?

2. Review what Jesus says about the Holy Spirit in the Upper Room Discourse. Reflect on your own life and whether you view the Holy Spirit in the same way that Jesus does.

3. Talk about the concept of "abiding in Christ." It is a little difficult to define clearly, so take your time. What does it mean to "abide"? What are some practical ways that it shows itself? Reflect on your own life in relation to this concept.

4. Jesus prays for unity among believers. What, in your experience, aids unity? What hurts unity?

5. Jesus says that his followers would be defined by their love for one another. How do you define love? What would this look like?

6. List some ways that you can be a servant leader in some areas of your life. Be concrete and specific.

7. In the Upper Room Discourse, is Jesus teaching the ordinance of foot washing or giving an example of humble servanthood that we should emulate? Why do you think so? If we should not practice foot washing, is there another modern equivalent that we should practice?

8. Define the Holy Spirit. Is the Holy Spirit a he or an it? How is the Holy Spirit related to God, God the father, and God the Son?

9. Give some specifics as to what it looks like to be "in" but not "of" the world.

10. Please spend some serious and lengthy time talking about this unity issue. What does it practically look like? How is it really possible for Christian unity to be evangelistic? Have you ever seen this happen? Have you ever seen just the reverse happen? What is it like for believers to be united the same way that the godhead is united?

14

Acts 1-12

I. INTRODUCTION

II. STRUCTURAL OVERVIEW

III. THE BIRTH AND EXPANSION OF THE EARLY CHURCH (ACTS 1-5)

   A. The First Forty Days (Acts 1)

   Choosing the twelfth disciple and a repeat of the promise of the coming Holy Spirit.

B. Pentecost (Acts 2)

1. The Coming of the Holy Spirit and Speaking in Tongues

The Holy Spirit came to dwell in individual believers in a permanent way.

2. Joel's Prophecy

Everyone who calls on the name of the Lord will be saved.

3. Language Used for the Coming of the Holy Spirit

Descriptions of the initial experience of the Holy Spirit being given and descriptions of the coming of the Holy Spirit in the ongoing experience of a Christian.

C. Peter's Sermon

Four basic elements are Jesus' life, crucifixion of Jesus, resurrection of Jesus and a call to repentance. This is referred to as the kerygma.

1. The Story Continues

2. Boldness (Acts 4:19-20, 29-31)

The church prayed for boldness to communicate the gospel in the hostile environment they faced. Your personal testimony can be powerful.

3. The Sovereignty of God (Acts 2:23,39; 4:27-38)

God is in charge.

4. Additional Stories

People in the church shared with each other. Some were beaten for telling others about Jesus and they considered it an honor to suffer.

IV. THE SECOND PHASE OF THE CHURCH'S EXPANSION: SAMARITANS (ACTS 6-9)

Do You Have to be a Jew to be a Christian?

The first theological battle in the church was how Gentile Christians and Jewish Christians would live and worship together.

A. Stephen (Acts 6-7)

Stephen recounts that the Jewish nation has a history of rejecting God's servants and refers to the Jewish leaders as, "stiff-necked" and "resisting the

B. Philip in Samaria (Acts 8)

Philip went to a non-Jewish area to preach the gospel and people there believed.

The Delay of Receiving the Holy Spirit

The believers in Samaria received the Holy Spirit when leaders of the Jewish church came to meet with them.

C. Saul (Acts 9)

Saul's conversion was an important event in the history of the early church.

V. THE THIRD PHASE OF THE CHURCH'S EXPANSION: GENTILES (ACTS 10-11)

A. Peter and Cornelius (Acts 10:1-11:18)

Peter's vision and interaction with Cornelius shows that the Gospel is meant for the Gentiles as well as the Jews.

B. The Church in Antioch

Antioch becomes the center of the Gentile church.

C. Closing

The Gospel is for all people.

Questions

1. Have you ever been "filled" with the Spirit in the sense of Acts 4:8? Explain what it was like. Reflect generally on the Spirit's filling in your own life.

2. How do you feel about the "sovereignty of God"? Many people have bad past experiences. If you are one of those people, what do you think of the verses discussed that show that God is in control? Is there any comfort in this biblical teaching for you?

3. Isn't it amazing how something like persecution can work to spread the gospel? Probably in the midst of the persecution, people did not understand why God was allowing this, although for us it is obvious. Is there anything in your own life that is difficult to understand, and yet there is the possibility that God will use it for his glory and the benefit of the church?

4. In Acts 2, Peter proclaims that the Spirit is poured out on all people, and throughout the rest of Acts, the Spirit comes to Jews, Samaritans, and Gentiles. Reflect on whether the church today views the Spirit as being poured out on all sorts of people.

5. With Pentecost, the Holy Spirit came in a permanent way. Do you live as if the Spirit is with you and filling you daily?

6. If you tell someone that they need to repent, and they say, "Repent of what?," what will you tell them?

7. What is the purpose of tongues in Acts 1-12? Resist the temptation to move into a discussion of the spiritual gifts of tongues for the time being. Is there any modern analogy you can think of to tongues?

8. What are the four points of the kerygma? How will you use this in your evangelism?

9. What was the church's first theological battle? Can you think of any modern parallels?

10. Reflect on the explanation of the delay in the giving of the Holy Spirit to the Samaritans make sense. Do you think this is a normative experience?

15

Acts 13-15 and Galatians

I. **ACTS 13-14: PAUL'S FIRST MISSIONARY JOURNEY**

   A. **Commission (Acts 13:1-3)**

   The church in Antioch commissioned Barnabas and Saul to go out and preach the gospel.

   B. **Cyprus (Acts 13:4-12)**

   Saul is called Paul from now on. The Roman governor believed their message.

C. Pisidian Antioch (Acts 13:13-52)

When you believe in Jesus, you receive forgiveness for your sins and it releases you from the burden of the law.

D. Iconium (Acts 14:1-7)

Barnabas and Paul face opposition from Jews who are not Christians.

E. Lystra and Derbe (Acts 14:8-20)

Paul healed a crippled man, causing the people to think that Barnabas and Paul are Greek gods.

F. Return through Lystra and Iconium to Antioch (Acts 14:21-28)

Paul reminded the believers that they will face persecution and conflict.

II. GALATIANS

A. Background

After Paul preached, Jews told the new Christians that they still needed to follow the Jewish Law and they were questioning Paul's authority.

B. Introduction: Curse rather than Blessing (Gal. 1:1-10)

Paul curses the people that were preaching a gospel that was different from the one he preached.

C. Paul's Apostleship (Gal. 1:11-2:14)

Paul defends his apostleship.

D. Triumph of Grace over Law (Gal. 2:15-4:7)

We are justified by faith in Christ, not by works of the law.

1. Definition of Justification and Righteousness

Justification is a legal term describing how God's righteousness is imputed to us.

2. Not by Works of the Law

Legalism is the opposite of salvation by faith.

3. The Doctrine of Justification by Faith

We are justified because we believe Jesus is God and because of what he did on the cross.

E. Crucified with Christ (Gal. 2:20)

We have died to our old way of living and we now live a life characterized by faith.

F. Freedom in Christ (Gal. 5:1-6:10)

The way we live should change because of our relationship with God.

G. Live by the Spirit (Gal. 5:16, 22-24)

We can live our lives being led by the Spirit because he gives us the power to do it.

H. New Creation (Gal. 6:15)

Because of our relationship to God, he makes us a new creation.

I. **The Message of Galatians**

We have been made right by God because we believe that Jesus is who he says he is and because of what he did on the cross, and we should live our lives accordingly.

III. **ACTS 15: JERUSALEM COUNCIL**

   A. **Background: The Debate (Acts 15:1-5)**

   One of the first theological questions of the church was, "Must I be a Jew to be a Christian?"

   B. **The Council's Decision and Letter (Acts 15:6-35)**

   Discussion about how the Jews and Gentiles can fellowship in the church.

   Probably written before the Jerusalem Council recorded in Acts 15.

Questions

1. The early church was very aware of the leading the Holy Spirit, and accompanied his leading with prayer and fasting. Have you ever experienced something like this?

2. Acts 13:12 says that the proconsul saw the miracles, was astonished at the teaching, and believed the gospel. The miracles got his attention but they were not the focus of his faith. Have you ever been astonished at the teaching of the gospel? What led to the experience? What was the long-term effects?

3. Have you ever acted like Peter? Have you ever known the right thing to do, but due to legalistic pressures given in? Why did you? What were the short-term and long-term effects of your actions?

4. How have you seen legalism creep back into a Christian's life and try to take it over? Was the legalist happy or sad? How can you help them see the difference between living by faith and living by works of the law?

5. In your own culture, what would be similar to the four prohibitions in the letter written by the Jerusalem church? What activities would you voluntarily abstain from if it aided the spread of the gospel?

6. The gospel frees people from the law; it is a result of God's grace. And yet, people so often prefer to fall back into law, into legalism. Discuss why you think this is the case.

7. Role play, explain "justification by faith" in your own words to a child, an adult non-Christian, and a person who tends toward legalism.

8. Do the same with "works of the law."

9. How would you explain the concept of being "crucified with Christ" in your own words? (Galatians 2:20)

10. Discuss the difference between walking by the Spirit and living legalistically.

11. Discuss whether you think the Judaizers in Acts 15 were Christians?

16

Acts 15:36-18:22 and 1-2 Thessalonians

I. PAUL'S SECOND MISSIONARY JOURNEY (ACTS 15:36-18:22)

   A. Context

   The conclusion of the Jerusalem Council in Acts 15 is that you are not required to be Jewish to be a Christian.

B. Disagreement over Mark

Paul and Barnabas disagree about whether or not they should take Mark with them on their next missionary journey. They decide to separate, so Paul takes Silas and Barnabas takes Mark.

C. Asia Minor and Timothy (Acts 16:1-10)

Paul and Silas meet Timothy and take him with them.

D. Philippi (Acts 16:11-40)

Philippi was a colony of Rome so you had the same rights and privileges you would if you were living in Rome.

E. The Conversion of Lydia (Acts 16:11-15)

When Paul preached, Lydia believed his message and she was baptized.

F. An Exorcism

Paul cast a demon out of a young woman slave. Her masters couldn't make money off her anymore, so they threw Paul and Silas in prison.

G. The Conversion of the Philippian Jailer

Paul and Silas were miraculously released from prison but stayed to present the gospel to the jailer.

H. Thessalonica (Acts 17:1-9)

Paul preached in the synagogue, then the Jews started a riot to protest what he was saying.

I. Berea (Acts 17:10-15)

When Paul left, Silas and Timothy stayed to disciple the new believers.

J. Athens (Acts 17:16-34)

Paul spoke on Mars Hill and presented Jesus by using the imagery of their idol to an unknown God.

K. Corinth (Acts 18:1-17)

The people in the synagogue did not accept Paul's preaching so he started preaching next door to the synagogue and stayed there for a year and a half.

L. Return to Antioch (Acts 18:18-22)

Paul stops in Ephesus and Jerusalem on his way back to Antioch.

II. 1 THESSALONIANS

Paul wrote this letter to encourage new believers that were facing persecution.

A. Background

B. Greeting and Thanksgiving (1 Thess. 1)

Paul greets the believers in Thessalonica and is thankful they they responded to the message of the gospel.

C. Paul Reviews his Time with Them (1 Thess. 2)

Paul reminds them that while he was there, he loved, served and encouraged them.

D. Paul Sent Timothy (1 Thess. 3)

Paul was writing the letter in Corinth and Timothy brought it to Thessalonica.

E. The Necessity of Christian Education

It's important for new believers to know that it's normal to experience persecution and conflict as they begin to live out their faith.

F. The Necessity of Persecution

Jesus and believers before us experienced persecution and if we live our lives being led by the Spirit, we will, too.

G. The Necessity of Perseverance

Perseverance is an essential aspect of our relationship with God.

H. Responding to Timothy's Report (1 Thess. 4-5)

Core Topics for a Young Church (1 Thess. 4:1-12)

The importance of hard work and sexual purity are two topics that Paul addresses in 1 Thessalonians.

I. Eschatology (1 Thess. 4:13-5:11)

Knowing that we will be with God forever is a great encouragement. We should be ready for Jesus' coming anytime.

J. Conclusion

Rejoice always, pray without ceasing, give thanks, do not quench the Spirit, abs

III. 2 THESSALONIANS

A. Persevere in the Face of Persecution (2 Thess. 1:5-12)

Our prayers for our enemies should be that they repent and become Christians.

B. Jesus's Return is Future (2 Thess. 2)

Persevere in your faith because Jesus is coming back again.

C. Idleness (2 Thess. 3)

If anyone is not willing to work, don't pay their way.

Questions

1. Have you ever had a sharp disagreement with a fellow Christian that appeared to be unsolvable, like Paul and Barnabas? We don't know much about their separation, but what was it that made your situation so difficult? As you look back on it, especially if it happened some time in the past, was God able to work anything good in the midst of your troubles? (We will learn the resolution of Paul's and Barnabas' conflict later in the New Testament.)

2. Have you ever voluntary limited your Christian liberty and freedom for the sake of the spread of the gospel? What were the circumstances behind it and the consequences stemming from it? Would you do it again?

3. Have you had any experience with household conversions? What led to it? Who played the father's role of being the first to hear and believe? How did it affect the others in the household? Are there any lessons you learned from this experience?

4. Nobody likes suffering and persecution, and yet we all recognize that in some form it promotes Christian growth. Share your stories as encouragement for others.

5. Rather than arguing about the rapture and the suddenness of Jesus's return, ask yourself if you are ready. What does this readiness look like?

6. When is civil disobedience appropriate and inappropriate? What are some improper motives leading to civil disobedience?

7. Reflect on Paul's speech in Athens. In your own context, what are some ways that you can use common ground to engage others in talking about God? Is it possible to go too far in looking for common ground? How can you also ensure that you are being bold and faithful?

8. Paul's pattern is that he preaches the gospel, then prioritizes Christian education. Brainstorm some ways that you or your community can practically do the same.

9. In light of 2 Thess. 3, discuss how you distinguish between lazy people who should not have the church's help, and others who for legitimate reasons are not able to make a living.

10. Church discipline is a difficult topic, especially in a culture that does not have house churches but rather has larger churches where people do not know each other. Discuss whether ostracizing Christians from the community works in our context.

17

Acts 18:23-21:26 and 1 Corinthians 1-6

Paul's Third Missionary Journey

I. **EPHESUS (ACTS 18:23-19:41)**

   A. Apollos (Acts 18:23-29)

   > Apollos was preaching the baptism of John the Baptist until Priscilla and Acquila explained the gospel to him.

B. Disciples of John the Baptist (Acts 19:1-7)

Paul preached the Gospel to them and they accepted it.

C. Paul's Ministry in Ephesus (Acts 19:8-20)

Paul used Ephesus as a central base for more than two years.

D. Writing of 1 Corinthians in Ephesus

Paul writes to the church he planted in Corinth regarding some problems he heard about there.

E. Riot in Ephesus (Acts 19:21-41)

A silversmith that made idols of Artemis started a riot against Paul because as people believed the gospel, they bou=ght fewer idols.

II. TRAVEL TOWARD JERUSALEM (ACTS 20:1-21:14)

Paul travels back toward Jerusalem by going through Corinth and collects donations along the way to help the church in Judea.

A. Writing of 2 Corinthians in Macedonia

Paul stops in Macedonia and writes 2 Corinthians there.

B. Writing of Romans in Corinth

Paul stays about 3 months in Corinth and writes his letter to the Romans.

C. Return to Jerusalem (Acts 20:3b-6)

On his way to Jerusalem, he stops at the seaport of Miletus to say goodbye to the Ephesian elders.

III. 1 CORINTHIANS

A. Commentaries

The commentary by Craig Blomberg is written for lay level study and one by Gordon Fee has more technical information.

B. Historical Background

Corinth was a large city, highly commercialized with a large temple that emphasized worship involving prostitutes.

C. Structural Overview

In the first half, Paul responds to information from a member of the church named Chloe. The second have is evidently a response to a letter with questions that the Corinthians sent Paul.

D. Divisions in the Church (1 Cor. 1:10-4:21)

People in the church were following personality cults rather than focusing on the message of the gospel.

1. Lack of Focus on Jesus

Paul wants the church to be unified and focusing on the preaching of what Jesus did on the cross.

2. Human Wisdom vs. Divine Wisdom

The foolishness of God is wiser than men.

3. Unity

The gospel is the vehicle by which the Spirit works in their lives to bring them into relationship to God and helps them understand the things of the Spirit.

4. Practical Issues Regarding Division in the Church

Genuinely love and be willing to serve each other in practical ways.

E. Moral Issues (1 Cor. 5-6)

1. Sexual Immorality (1 Cor. 5)

If someone is living an immoral lifestyle in your community of faith, it's important to deal with it.

2. Church Discipline

The goal of church discipline is restoration.

Questions

1. In 1 Cor. 1-4, Paul confronts the celebrity mentality of the church and points people to celebrate Jesus alone as their leader. Have you experienced this kind of celebrity mentality in church, where people gather behind a leader rather than Jesus? What are some of the consequences of this? What are some solutions for the church to correct this mentality?

2. Brainstorm some of the ways in which divine wisdom differs from human or worldly wisdom. What stands out to you personally as highly significant?

3. Have you or someone else you know been hurt by the church to the point of leaving? Was it possible and/or appropriate to maintain any unity in the midst of this? Reflect on how this affected the overall witness of the church in the community.

4. Scan 1 Cor. 5-6. Are there any sins listed that you are dealing with presently (or have dealt with in the past) in your heart or actions? Remember that God's heart for discipline is always restoration. What steps can you take in your own restoration now?

5. In light of Matthew 18, is there another Christian that you have something against or who has something against you? Ask God if there is some action you can take to seek them out.

6. Have you ever experienced a church carrying out church discipline? What was it like? Did anything positive come from it?

7. God desires there to be unity among his people (1 John 17, 1 Cor. 1-4). Write out or pray a prayer for unity in your specific context. Then, reflect on what your specific role in creating unity within the body is. What, practically, can you do?

8. Discuss when, if ever, disunity is appropriate in the church.

9. Identify the benefits and detriments of the church having so many different denominations.

10. The cultural context is different today than in the ancient world. Discuss how church discipline does and doesn't work in our church context today, especially in terms of sexual immorality. How should the church practice this? Is there any sense in which the church ought to modify church discipline?

11. Practice confronting a Christian friend who is struggling with a specific sin that Paul mentions in 1 Cor. 5-6. How can you lovingly and firmly help them? Keep in mind that God wants their restoration.

18

1 Corinthians 7-16 and 2 Corinthians

1 Corinthians

I. **MARRIAGE (1 COR. 7)**

   A. **Asceticism (1 Cor. 7:1-7)**

   If you are married, don't neglect the sexual needs of your marriage partner.

   B. **Unmarried (1 Cor. 7:8-9)**

   If you are unmarried or widow, it's ok to marry, but in some ways, it's better to stay single if you have the gift of celibacy.

C. Married (1 Cor. 7:10-11)

If you are married, stay married.

D. Mixed Marriages (1 Cor. 7:12-16)

Stay married if you can. Let the unbelieving spouse leave if they want to.

E. General principle (1 Cor. 7:17-24)

Each person should lead the life God has called them to.

F. Engaged (1 Cor. 7:25-35)

Paul's preference is to stay single to focus on serving the Lord.

G. Death and Remarriage (1 Cor. 7:39-40)

If your spouse dies, you are free to remarry.

H. Legitimate Reasons for Divorce

God designed marriage to be for life,

I. Remarriage

Passages that teach about divorce, remarriage and forgiveness.

II. FOOD OFFERED TO IDOLS (1 COR. 8)

The question of voluntarily limiting your freedom in situations that might cause someone to fundamentally question their faith.

III. WORSHIP (1 COR. 11:2-14:40)

A. Men and Women Relationships (1 Cor. 11:2-16)

Live in such a way that you honor the relationships you have in your family and your church.

B. The Lord's Supper (1 Cor. 11:17-34)

Partake in communion to remember what God has done for you, reflect on your relationship with God and others, and look forward to his coming again.

C. Spiritual Gifts (1 Cor. 12-14)

Exercise the spiritual gift that God gives you for the common good of your faith community.

IV. THE RESURRECTION (1 COR. 15)

Christ's resurrection is central to our faith. We will also receive a physical resurrection body.

V. THE INTERMEDIATE STATE (2 COR 5)

Discussion of what happens to our soul when we die and when we receive our resurrected body.

Questions

1. Do we live in a sense of urgency that the Lord could return quickly, without warning? When you think about Jesus returning any time, how does this change how you think about life?

2. Can you share any examples of mixed marriages in which the nonbeliever eventually became a Christian? Was this "missionary dating," where a Christian married someone in hopes that they would become a Christian, or did one person become a Christian after marriage? Reflect on this example in light of Scripture. What conclusions can you draw about God's heart in this?

3. In light of 1 Cor. 11:2-16. Reflect on the concept of authority and submission among the persons of the trinity and within the church. What personally affects you? What questions, concerns, or beliefs do you hold?

4. In your experience, how has the exercise of spiritual gifts divided the church? How have they united? Do you have any examples of spiritual gifts exercised without love? Have you ever seen the gifts of tongues and interpretation used effectively as a witness to non-believers in the church situation? What about the reverse?

5. What do you think it is going to be like in heaven? What will it be like to be a disembodied spirit? Will we be able to touch each other? Reflect on what Judgment Day is going to be like when we come with Christ and are raised with our glorified bodies.

6. How do you feel overall in reference to Paul's basic tenet in 1 Cor. 7 that celibacy is "better" than marriage? Reflect on this, but then also come up with some practical things our churches can do to communicate this better.

7. Come up with and answer for a some who asks about whether it is God's will for them or their child to marry their non-Christian fiancé. How would you be both gentle and yet firm?

8. Come up with your position on what you believe are legitimate reasons for divorce. Think through some different scenarios—abuse, emotional abandonment, pornography use, etc.

9. In light of 1 Cor. 8, discuss some areas in which Christians are free to exercise their Christian freedom but perhaps should limit it for the sake of others. Then, discuss at what point, if any, this principle becomes a license for the "weaker" Christian to control others. Have you ever had someone tell you that you were causing them to stumble, and really all that you were doing was bugging them and their religious traditions? Share what you did.

10. In 1 Cor. 11, Paul discusses how men's and women's hairstyles signal their relationship status with each other and God. Since hairstyles no longer mean the same thing for us, what are some of those signs in our own culture?

19

Romans 1-4

I. **INTRODUCTION**

   A. **Commentaries**

      Broadman and Holman by Robert Mounce, Baker by Tom Schreiner, Eerdmans by Douglas Moo.

   B. **Historical Setting**

      Written at the end of Paul's third missionary journey. It's the most systematic presentation of biblical theology in the Bible.

C. Structural Overview

Chapters 1-4 focus primarily on sin and salvation, chapters 5-8 on sanctification, chapters 9-11 on Jews and their relationship to Gentiles and God's overall plan, and chapters 12-16 on ethics.

II. INTRODUCTION TO THE BOOK OF ROMANS (ROM. 1:1-15)

Paul identifies himself and greets his audience which is the people in Rome.

III. THEME VERSES (ROM. 1:16-17)

The gospel is the power of God for salvation and the righteous will live by faith.

A. The Power of the Gospel (Rom. 1:16)

The gospel is powerful even though it seems weak to the world. It came to the Jews first, then to everyone else.

B. The Essential Nature of the Gospel (Rom. 1:17)

Faith is being fully convinced that God is able to do the very thing that he has promised he would do.

C. Old Testament Proof (Hab. 2:4; 3:17-19)

The righteous will live by faith.

IV. THE UNRIGHTEOUSNESS OF ALL PEOPLE (ROM. 1:18-3:20)

Everyone apart from Christ is unrighteous.

A. The Gentiles, Who Have General Revelation (Rom. 1:18-32)

There are universal truths that God has made known to all people.

B. The Jews, Who Have the Law (Rom. 2:1-3:8)

It's not enough to be born into a Jewish family. Your life must be changed.

C. Summary and Scriptural Proof (Rom. 3:9-20)

All have sinned. We can't make ourselves right with God by our own efforts.

V. RIGHTEOUSNESS DEFINED: JUSTIFICATION (ROM. 3:21-4:25)

A. Justification is Through Christ (Rom. 3:21-26)

1. Relation of Justification to the Law (Rom. 3:21)

The righteousness of God has been manifested apart from the Law, although the Law and the Prophets bear witness to it.

2. **Through Faith in Christ for All (Rom. 3:22-25a)**

   We are justified by God's grace and he redeems us.

3. **Hilasterion (Propitiation; Expiation)**

   Christ's death of the cross appeases God's wrath toward our sin.

4. **The Justice of God's Actions (Rom. 3:25b-26)**

   The death of Jesus was necessary for God to be just and also forgive your sins.

5. **Justification is through Faith (Rom. 3:27-4:25)**

B. Abraham was Justified by Faith (Rom. 4:1-8)

Abraham was forgiven because of his faith and trust in God, just like we are.

C. Abraham was not Justified by Circumcision (Rom. 4:9-12)

Abraham is the father of all who believe, including the Gentiles, because he had faith in God before he was circumcised.

D. The Promise is by Faith (Rom. 4:13-17a)

It applies to anyone, not only people with a certain ethnic heritage or religious activity.

E. Description of Abraham's Faith and Application (Rom. 4:17b-25)

God gives life to the dead and calls into existence the things that do not exist.

Questions

1. Reflect on whether there are any areas of your life in which you live as though you are justified by works. What can you do to change this?

2. Why isn't Paul ashamed of the Gospel? (Rom. 1:16-17) Identify some of the reasons that people are ashamed of the Gospel today, and respond to each of these reasons.

3. Has God ever been patient with you, giving you time to repent? How did you feel afterwards when you look back over your time of sin?

4. Reflect on the idea that God passed over the sins committed beforehand, and that through Jesus, he demonstrates his justice at the present time. What is the connection between Jesus's death on the cross and God's character as a just God?

5. What is the balance between not being justified by works (Rom. 4), but good works still being important in God's eyes (Rom. 4:6-8)? How do you or can you maintain this own balance in your own life?

6. In light of Romans 1, discuss the ways that God has made himself known to the world. How does this practically affect the way would talk to an unbeliever about God?

7. What does justification by works look like today? What might correspond to possessing the law and circumcision today? How would you explain justification by faith in light of the modern examples of justification by works?

8. How would you define "faith" to a person who has never stepped foot in a church?

9. How would you explain what Jesus did on the cross using hilasterion?

10. Summarize the argument about Abraham's faith that Paul makes in Romans 4.

20

Romans 5-11

VI. RIGHTEOUSNESS LIVED OUT (ROM. 5-8)

A. The Christian's Joy (Rom. 5:1-21)

The benefits of knowing for sure that we are justified.

1. Description of the Benefits (Rom. 5:1-11)

We are at peace with God, we can rejoice even when circumstances are difficult, our hope is secure.

2. **Sufficiency of Christ's Sacrifice (Rom. 5:12-21)**

   Jesus' death on the cross is sufficient to cover our sins.

B. **Moral Implications of Justification: Sanctification (Rom. 6)**

   Sanctification is our growth toward being like Christ.

   1. **Dead to Sin but Alive with Christ (Rom. 6:1-14)**

      Since the mastery of sin over your life is gone, live like a different person.

   2. **Slaves to Christ (Rom. 6:15-23)**

      You are either a slave to sin or a slave to righteousness.

C. Freedom from the Law's Condemnation (Rom. 7:1-25)

We struggle with sin, but God gives us the power to overcome it and forgives us when we fail.

D. The Work of the Holy Spirit (Rom. 8:1-39)

The Holy Spirit lives in us and is at work with the same power that raised Jesus from the dead.

1. The Indwelling of the Holy Spirit (Rom. 8:1-17)

As we respond to the leading of the Spirit in our lives, we change the way we think and act.

2. Future Hope of the Believer (Rom. 8:18-30)

God can redeem any situation we face to help us become more like Jesus.

3. Summation: The Justification and Love of God (Rom. 8:31-39)

We can never be separated from the love of God.

VII. RIGHTEOUSNESS VINDICATED (JEW AND GENTILE QUESTION) (ROM. 9-11)

How is it that the Jews rejected Jesus even though they knew about the promises God made to Abraham?

A. The Justice of the Rejection (Rom. 9:6-29)

1. A Remnant Still Exists, by Election (Rom. 9:6-13)

God knew that not all Jews would accept Jesus as Messiah but that there would be a remnant who would.

2. **God's Sovereignty is Righteous (Rom. 9:14-29)**

   Sometimes we don't understand why God does things the way he does, but that doesn't mean that he is unfair. Our perspective is limited and God's is not.

   a) **Double Predestination**

      Some people believe that God chose people to respond to him and that he chose others to reject him.

   b) **Issues in Election**

      If you can't say, "no," then you really didn't say, "yes," and it challenges our doctrine of justice.

B. The Cause of the Rejection (Rom. 9:30-10:21)

The Jews rejected Jesus because they pursued righteousness by works, not by faith.

C. A Future for Ethnic Israel (Rom. 11:25-26)

These verses indicate that there is a future for ethnic Israel in God's redemptive plan.

D. Closing: The Unsearchable Depth of God's Wisdom (Rom. 11:33)

There are some things that we will not completely understand about God because of our limited perspective.

Questions

1. In Romans 5, Paul writes, "Therefore, since we have been justified by faith, we have peace with God through our Lord Jesus Christ." This peace is a reality, but sometimes we don't feel at peace. Is there an area of your where you need to believe you are at peace with God? Meditate on this passage.

2. Have you ever rejoiced in the midst of difficult times because you knew what was being formed in yourself (Rom. 5:3-4)? How would our handling of difficult times be transformed if we could believe these verses in the midst of the pain? Is it possible?

3. We can have complete confidence that our hope is secure because, Christ didn't die for us because we were doing a good job. Paul says, "God shows his love for us in that while we were still sinners, Christ died for us." Reflect on this passage personally, and assess whether there are areas of your life that need to be transformed by this truth.

4. Talk about sin for a while. Are you increasing in your awareness of your own sin? How does it make you feel? What does it drive you to do? What does it look like in practical terms to think of sin as a foreign object in your body trying to destroy you, even though you are still responsible for your sin? Is it encouraging or discouraging to know that you will always struggle with sin?

5. What are your reflections on the idea of election presented in the lecture from Romans 9-11? What is difficult to understand? What are the most convincing answers so far?

6. In Romans 5, Paul writes, "3 Not only that, but we rejoice in our sufferings, knowing that suffering produces endurance, 4 and endurance produces character, and character produces hope." What is the logic of this passage? Why does each one produce the next?

7. In Romans 6, Paul essentially says, "You've died to sin, so live like it, this is who you are!" Sin is not to have an ongoing role in our life. What can we learn from this statement about the relationship between identity and action? How can you implement this principle in your own life and in your speech to others? Come up with a practical plan of action.

8. Your friend thinks that even though he is a Christian, that he is free to do whatever he wants. After all, God will just forgive him. How do you answer this? What are the right motivations you for him not to continue in sin, and how could you help foster these?

9. Explain to a new believer how Romans 6—we have died to sin—and Romans 7—sin will continue to be a struggle—can be harmonized. What does this mean for their new life in Christ?

10. Slowly read through Romans 8 and pick out a verse that brings you the most encouragement or security. Commit this verse to memory.

11. Create an outline of the argument of Romans 9 in your own words.

21

Romans 9-16

Review of the Structure of Romans

Apart from Christ, everyone is a sinner, it is possible to be right with God because of Jesus' death on the cross, we are at peace with God, the Holy Spirit leads us in the process of sanctification, and salvation history includes both Jews and Gentiles.

VIII. RIGHTEOUSNESS LIVED OUT (ROM. 12-15)

    A. The Relationship Between Theology and Ethics

        What we believe should make a difference in how we act.

B. **Responsibility to God: Be Transformed (Rom. 12:1-2)**

Spiritual formation.

1. **Our Motivation (v. 1a)**

    We grow in our faith in response to the mercies of God.

2. **Present ALL of Yourself to God as a Sacrifice (v. 1b)**

    There is no room for compartmentalization of our thoughts or actions.

3. **Refuse to Be Like the World (v. 2a)**

    The mold of the world is powerful and seduces many people.

4. Insist on Following God's Will (v. 2b)

The Holy Spirit will transform us if we follow his leading.

C. Responsibility to the Church (Rom. 12:3-21)

Our growth in humility should express itself in unity and genuine love for those in your faith community.

D. Responsibility to the Government (Rom. 13:1-7)

Our duty is to obey the civil authorities because God has put them there.

1. The Question of Civil Disobedience

There are times for civil disobedience.

2. How Do You Decide? Ethical Hierarchy

Our allegiance to God and other people is primary.

E. Responsibility to Society (Rom. 13:8-14)

We should live in a way that demonstrates how to love God and others.

F. Responsibility of the Weak and the Strong (Rom. 14:1-15:13)

1. Issue of weak and strong people and causing people to stumble.

Two Groups of People

Mostly Jews who had stricter dietary laws than the gentiles.

2. Opinion and Adiaphora

Some areas of faith and practice deal with secondary issues on which believers may have different opinions.

3. Causing Another to "Stumble"

Stumbling means you are leading someone to sin, not just annoying them because of their preferences.

4. Instructions to the Weak and the Strong

Don't pass judgment or despise others, but build each other up.

5. Instructions Specifically for the Strong

Don't quarrel over opinions. Sometimes it's better to limit your freedom for the sake of the church and the glory of God.

IX. EPISTOLARY CONCLUSION (ROM. 15:14-16:27)

Summary of his travel plans and greetings to people he knows that are currently in Rome.

Questions

1. What is the meaning of "Therefore," in Rom. 12:1? What is Paul referring to, and what implication does this have?

2. In what ways does the world seek to mold us into its image? How do we resist conforming to the patterns of the world (Rom. 12:1), but also still care for the world?

3. What is your primary motivation for life change, for obedience, for striving to learn? What have you understood from Paul in Romans that it should be? How can you change or foster this in your life?

4. In Romans 14, Paul says, "But put on the Lord Jesus Christ, and make no provision for the flesh, to gratify its desires." In other words, don't even plan to be able to sin, don't set yourself up in a situation to where you may be able to get away with sinning. Reflect on this verse and how it relates to your own life.

5. Have you ever seen someone use the argument that another is causing them to stumble by doing something? What did they mean by "stumble"? Did this accord with what Paul is saying in Romans 14?

6. Explain the argument of Romans chapter by chapter. Does the argument make sense? Is there any part that needs clarification still?

7. Discuss when civil disobedience is appropriate and inappropriate. Do you think our general tendency is to dismiss Romans 13 and not believing that the government is a God ordained authority? In light of Romans 13's encouragement to give more respect to government authorities, how can we respond? What does this practically look like?

8. Paul says in Romans 13: "You shall love your neighbor as yourself." 10 Love does no wrong to a neighbor; therefore, love is the fulfilling of the law." Explain to a new believer in what way love fulfills the Old Testament law.

9. In Romans 14 and 15, Paul speaks of voluntary limitations of our freedom for the sake of the church and the Glory of God. Come up with some practical examples of this today.

10. Paul says don't pass judgment or despise the other person. 14:3: "Let not the one who eats despise the one who abstains, and let not the one who abstains pass judgment on the one who eats, for God has welcomed him." Is this difficult to do? Use some of the examples from the prior question.

22

Acts 21:27-28:31 and Ephesians

I. **ACTS 21:27-28:31**

   Paul's imprisonment and series of trials on his way to Rome.

   A. **Mob, Arrest, and Defense (Acts 21:27-22:29)**

      Paul enters the temple with a person that people think, wrongly, is an uncircumcised Gentile. The protest becomes a mob and Paul is arrested.

B. **Four Trials: Sanhedrin, Felix, Festus, and Agrippa (Acts 22:30-26:32)**

The account of the trials is to show that Paul did not do anything wrong.

C. **Final Jewish Rejection (Acts 28:17-29)**

When Paul preached the gospel to the Jews in Rome, they rejected it.

II. EPHESIANS

A. **Introduction**

1. **Prison Epistles**

    Paul wrote of the New Testament letters when he was under house arrest in Rome.

2. Circular Letter

Ephesians was meant to be read by the believers in Ephesus and then circulated to other believers living in nearby cities.

3. Two-Fold Structure and Resources

The first three chapters focus on theology and the last three focus on ethics.

B. Part I: Theology (Eph. 1-3)

1. Our Spiritual Blessings (Eph. 1:3-14)

Paul lays out in detail some of the things that God has done for us.

a) Election (Eph. 1:4)

God chose you.

b) **Adoption (Eph. 1:5-6)**

God adopted us to be in relationship with him, so we are fellow-heirs with Jesus.

c) **Redemption (Eph. 1:7-10)**

Because of what Jesus did on the cross, our sins are forgiven.

d) **Inheritance (Eph. 1:11-12)**

God promises us an inheritance in heaven.

e) **Holy Spirit (Eph. 1:13-14)**

The Holy Spirit lives in us and helps us to persevere so we can receive our inheritance.

2. **Who We Are Individually in Christ (Eph. 2:1-10)**

    a) **Dead in Sin (Eph. 2:1-3)**

    Before our relationship with Jesus, we were dead in sin.

    b) **God Saved Us (Eph. 2:4-10)**

    God saved us by grace through faith to show his love for us.

    c) **Implications of God Saving Us**

    The more you understand how much God loves you and what you were saved from, the more you will want to live your life by God's power and leading.

3. **Who we are Corporately as the Church (Eph. 2:11-22)**

   Christ broke down the wall of hostility between the Jews and Gentiles.

4. **Closing Prayer for Spiritual Maturity (Eph. 3:14-21)**

   Paul's desire was that the people who believed the gospel that he preached would pursue spiritual maturity. Theology must always end in doxology.

C. **Part II: Ethics (Eph. 4-6)**

1. **Walk in Unity (Eph. 4:1-16)**

   Encouragement for the Jews and Gentiles to grow to maturity together.

2. **Walk in Holiness (Eph. 4:17-32)**

   Live a sanctified life. The image Paul uses is putting off your old self and putting on your new self.

3. **Walk in Love (Eph. 5:1-6)**

   Be imitators of God in the way you treat other people.

4. **Household Codes (Eph. 5:22-6:9)**

   Guidelines for how people within a family should relate to each other.

5. **Armor of God (Eph. 6:10-20)**

   The battle we face each day is against spiritual forces, so our armor must be spiritual, also.

Questions

1. Read through the spiritual blessings we have received in Christ (Eph. 1:3-14). Which one stands out to you as most significant, and why?

2. Reflect on the imagery of us all being "adopted" by God. What images or thoughts come to mind? How does this encourage you?

3. Do you think much about your heavenly inheritance? If not, why?

4. This whole idea of being "dead in sin" (Eph. 2) is a challenging idea for many to understand. Why is this hard for some people? Do you understand this passage in a different way?

5. What do you think about your spiritual battle, a battle not against "flesh and blood" but against evil spiritual powers. How does or should this affect your life?

6. How do we, in practical terms, bless God? (Eph. 1:3-14)

7. In light of the close connection between salvation and sanctification in Eph. 2:1-10, How are you going to describe the process of salvation to someone? Will you talk about sanctification?

8. What are some practical ways that we, like Paul in Eph. 3:20-21, can end our theology in doxology (proclamation and glorification of God)? What does this look like in your personal study, formal study, or church? What kind of practices can be implemented to make this connection stronger?

9. Spend some time thinking about "corrupting talk" (Eph. 5:1-6) This is an incredibly divisive and hurtful problem in the church and one that at times seems impossible to overcome. Are you prone to any sort of corrupting talk? What are you going to do about it? What do you think about Cymbala's comments?

10. The armor of God in Ephesians 6 sometimes seems to be unrelated to what comes prior. Examine this material and the prior chapter—can you identify a relationship?

23

Philippians

I. **INTRODUCTION**

    A. **Acts 16**

    Paul preached in Philippi on his second missionary journey. He baptized Lydia and explained the gospel to the jailer after Paul and Silas were miraculously freed from prison.

    B. **Purpose**

    The believers in Philippi sent him money to support his ministry so he wrote a letter to thank them.

C. Philippi

The city was a Roman colony with a predominately Greek culture. Possibly not even a synagogue there.

D. Commentaries

NIV series by Frank Thielman, Eerdmans by Gordon Fee.

II. SALUTATION (PHIL. 1:1-2)

Paul is under house arrest in Rome and Timothy is with him. He specifically references the overseers and deacons in Philippi.

III. THANKSGIVING AND PRAYER (PHIL. 1:3-11)

A. Paul's Affection for the Philippian Church

Paul had a strong emotional connection with the believers in the church in Philippi.

B. Paul's Prayer

Paul prays that the believers there will grow deeper in their walk with God

IV. IMPRISONMENT (PHIL. 1:12-26)

A. The Sovereignty of God in Spreading the Gospel (Phil. 1:12-18a)

The Jews tried to kill Paul to stop the spread of the gospel, but because he is now under house arrest in Rome, he can preach to the imperial guard, the household of Caesar, other people in Rome and write letters to people like the believers in Philippi.

B. Assurance of Innocence and Release (Phil. 1:18b-26)

Paul makes comments indicating the he is optimistic that he will soon be released.

V. CALL FOR UNITY (PHIL. 1:27-2:18)

Paul encouraged the believers in Philippi to have less rivalry and more unity

A. Goal of Unity (Phil. 1:27-30)

The goal is to be worthy of the gospel of Christ.

1. Indicative/Imperative

An indicative verb indicates a statement of fact. An imperative verb is a command.

2. Stand Firm in One Spirit

Do not waver in your commitment to Jesus or each other.

3. Two Consequences

We will strive together for the faith of the gospel and we will not be frightened by those who are persecuting us.

B. Call to Unity (Phil. 2:1-4)

1. Same mind

Because you are joined together with Christ, have the same mindset.

2. Same Love, One for Other

In humility, treat others as more significant than yourselves.

C. Example of Christ's Humility (Phil. 2:5-18)

1. Humiliation (Phil. 2:6-8)

Jesus was the exact representation of God. He became a human and put the needs of all people ahead of himself to the point that he died on the cross so everyone could be saved.

2. Exaltation (Phil. 2:9-11)

Because of Jesus' death, resurrection and ascension, he is declared Lord.

3. Consequences of the Truth (Phil. 2:12-18)

Work out what it means to live your life as a disciple of Jesus. Do it without grumbling, complaining, gossiping and slandering.

D. Personal Comments (Phil. 2:19-29)

Paul is sending Timothy and Epaphroditus back to Philippi with this letter.

E. Stand Firm in the Lord (Phil. 3:1-4:1)

Persevere in your faith.

F. Series of Admonitions

Don't worry. Set your mind on things that are true, honorable, just, pure lovely, commendable and excellent.

G. Being Content and Salutation (Phil. 4:1-23)

Be content.

Questions

1. What can we do to help remind ourselves that or citizenship is in heaven and that we should live our lives looking forward to the future and not consumed with the present?

2. Have you ever experienced God taking what someone intended for evil and turning it into good? Have you ever experienced someone preaching or teaching the gospel correctly but for the wrong motives? How might things have been different if the motives were good?

3. When we read Paul talking about his living solely for God and not himself, we need to realize that Paul is a mature Christian and this type of self-denial is the result of a long process. But having said that, what would it look like in your life to live this type of life? What would have to change?

4. Read through and reflect on Paul's teaching on rejoicing and anxiousness in Philippians 4:4-7. How does this impact your life?

5. The "Philippians 4:8 test" of thinking only on excellent of praiseworthy things is a challenge. Is it a good test? Give some specific examples of how it would apply to your lifestyle. What is it so hard to follow this "test"?

6. Paul continuously motivates behavior change by addressing identity, in other words, he reminds people who they are in Christ and then calls them to act like it. Identify a behavior in your own life that is contrary to the ways of God. What is the identity piece that would speak to that behavior? How can you implement a greater understanding of this truth in your own life daily?

7. Do the same as above, but for someone who you care about and have noticed behavior that is not Christlike. What is the piece of their true identity that they need to hear and understand? How can you play a part?

8. Unity is a difficult topic, but one that is obviously essential for a healthy Christian life. What did you learn about unity in Philippians that perhaps you did not grasp in our discussion in 1 Corinthians? What does "one mind" look like in your family and church?

9. How do you define "humility"? How could you explain to a young person that Jesus was the most humble man of all time while at the same time being God?

10. Explain in your own words what it means to "work out your salvation," giving full weight to the call to spiritual growth while protecting yourself of the charge of teaching works salvation.

24

Colossians and Philemon

I. **INTRODUCTION**

   A. Prison Epistles

   B. Colossians and Philemon.

   C. Commentaries

      NIV Application Series by Dave Garland, Eerdmans by F. F. Bruce, Tyndale New Testament Commentaries by N. T. Wright

D. Background on Colossians

Small agrarian town. Paul may have not been there but he evangelized Epaphras who was from there.

II. COLOSSIANS

A. Salutation, Thanksgiving, and Prayer (Col. 1:1-14)

Paul and his team were praying for spiritual maturity for the believers.

B. The Supremacy of Christ (Col. 1:15-20)

Paul emphasizes the Christology of Jesus, possibly because people in the Colossian church were downplaying or misrepresenting who he was.

1. **Jesus is Fully God**

    Jesus is the visible exact representation of the invisible God.

2. **Jesus is Firstborn**

    Possibly either an allusion to the supremacy of Jesus or to the fulfillment of the Old Testament prophecies about the coming Messiah.

3. **Jesus is Creator**

    Jesus created everything.

4. **Jesus is Pre-Existent**

    Jesus existed before all things.

5. Jesus is Sustainer

Everything holds together because of Jesus.

6. Jesus is Head of the Church

As believers we function under the authority of Jesus.

7. Jesus is Firstborn from the Dead

Jesus was the first to be raised from the dead to receive his glorified body and fully participate in the new age.

8. Jesus Reconciled All Things

Jesus is the one way that you come to peace with God.

C. Summary of Pauline Theology (Col. 1:21-23)

An explanation of how you become a disciple of Jesus and persevere in your faith.

D. Paul's Ministry to the Church (Col. 1:24-2:5)

Paul is glad for the chance to suffer for the cause of Christ so he can continue to encourage the believers in Colossae to grow in maturity in their faith.

E. Getting to the Issue at Hand (Col. 2:1-5)

Paul encourages the believers in Colossae to believe what he has taught them and not be swayed by false teaching that seems logical.

F. Colossian Heresy (Col. 2:6-23)

1. Spiritual Climate of Syncretism

It was common for the Roman and Greek religions to worship multiple gods and rely on superstitious practices.

2. Emphasis on Food Laws

The importance of food laws was often associated with people practicing Judaism.

3. Animism and Angel Worship

Belief in spirits and demons was common.

4. Solution to the Colossian Heresy (Col. 2:6-23)

Don't be deceived by philosophy and human tradition, and focus on the centrality of who Jesus is and what he did on the cross.

G. Ethical Instructions (Col. 3:1-4:6)

Paul uses the imagery of "putting off" some things so you can "put on" other things. He also talks about how people in families should act toward each other. He also talks about slavery in a way that became the see of the abolition movement.

III. PHILEMON

A. Philemon and Onesimus

Philemon was a wealthy person who owned Onesimus as a slave. Onesimus escaped to Rome and became a believer because of Paul.

B. Paul's "Appeal" to Philemon

Paul asks Philemon to forgive Onesimus and accept him back.

C. Slavery

1. Paul's Apparent Acceptance of Slavery

Paul does not explicitly denounce slavery.

2. Planting Seeds for the Abolition of Slaver

Paul asserts the equality of slave and master.

Questions

1. Read through Colossians 1:15-20. What impacts you the most? Why?

2. Paul makes one of the strongest statements about the doctrine of perseverance in Colossians 1:22-23: But now he has reconciled you by Christ's physical body through death to present you holy in his sight, without blemish and free from accusation— if you continue in your faith, established and firm, and do not move from the hope held out in the gospel. What are your beliefs about perseverance, and how do these sorts of verses make you feel?

3. In Colossians 1:28-29, Paul expresses the balance of human toil and God's power: "He is the one we proclaim, admonishing and teaching everyone with all wisdom, so that we may present everyone fully mature in Christ. To this end I strenuously contend with all the energy Christ so powerfully works in me." How can or do you maintain this same balance?

4. Have you heard people use Paul's caution against arguments and philosophy in Colossians 2 to argue that we should not study philosophy? What is your take on God's perspective toward such study?

5. In Colossians, Paul criticizes asceticism, the abstinence of any worldly pleasure and even severity toward the body. Do you or anyone else you know tend toward this kind of attitude? What can you do?

Lesson 24. Colossians and Philemon

6. Describe the spiritual climate of the Colossian culture. Are there any modern day parallels that you can think of? What would be Paul's advice?

7. In the hymn of the supremacy of Christ (Col. 1:15-20), Paul identifies various qualities of Jesus. How could you explain to someone using this passage that Jesus is God? What are all of the supports for that claim within this hymn?

8. Explain how the passage on the supremacy of Christ relates to the rest of the book of Colossians.

9. What is your assessment of Paul's comments about slavery? Is he pro-slavery? Against it? Are there other places in Scripture that apply to the topic of slavery?

10. Much like Jesus does for us, Paul "stands in the gap," so to speak, for Onesimus, telling Philemon "If he has done you any wrong or owes you anything, charge it to me" (v. 18). Is there anyone in your life that you can "stand in the gap" for? How can you defend someone or advocate for someone in need?

25

The Pastoral Epistles

I. BACKGROUND AND RESOURCES

Word Biblical Commentary by William Mounce, New International Biblical Commentary by Gordon Fee.

It's likely from reading 2 Timothy that Paul was released from house arrest in Rome, then later rearrested and put in a Roman prison.

II. 1 TIMOTHY

A. The Problems in Ephesus

Paul had warned them earlier that some of their elders come in later and lead them astray. Paul's solution is to remind Timothy that he knows sound doctrine and encourage him to stand up to false teachers.

B. Timothy

Paul was Timothy's spiritual father and they were good friends. 1 and 2 Timothy were written to encourage and instruct Timothy in his ministry in Ephesus.

C. How to Deal with Heresy

1. Teach Right Doctrine and Correct Error

Teach what is true about who Jesus is and what he did on the cross.

2. Teach Right Behavior

It's often true that people who teach heresy act in ways that are not Christ-like.

3. Be Willing to Confront

Paul encourages Timothy to not be quarrelsome, and correct his opponents with gentleness.

4. Avoid False Teachers after Warning Them

If a person stirs up division, warn them and then have nothing to do with them.

5. Recognize the Cause

These false teachers knew what they were teaching was wrong and they taught it anyway to gain wealth or power. Sometimes the problem is moral and not intellectual.

6. Watch Yourself in the Process

Watch your character as well as what you are teaching.

D. The Role of Women in Public Worship (1 Tim. 2:8-15)

1. Instruction to Men (1 Tim. 2:8)

    Men should pray without anger or quarreling.

2. Instruction to Women about Dress (1 Tim. 2:9-10)

    Women should adorn themselves in respectable apparel.

3. Women during the Teaching (1 Tim. 2:11-15)

    a) Quietly

    The word has the sense of, "quiet spirit."

b) **Submissiveness**

Doesn't say to whom, but most likely their husband or church leadership.

c) **I Do Not Permit a Woman to Teach…**

The question is to what situations does this apply?

4. **The Rationale (1 Tim. 2:14-15)**

The creation of Adam and Eve.

Additional Reading: Word Biblical Commentary by William Mounce, First Timothy 2:11-12 by Tom Schreiner, Recovering Biblical Manhood and Womanhood by Wayne Grudem and John Piper

E. Leadership Qualifications

It's sometimes difficult to determine how to put into practice the qualifications that Paul recommends for elders.

1. Character

Managing their household, time commitment.

2. Men Only

This is a debated topic but seems to be what the Bible means.

3. Oversight and Teaching Ability

General authority and the ability to rebuke false teaching.

4. Above Reproach

Fundamentally your life should show that you are living in a way that glorifies God.

5. A "One-Woman" Man

Faithfulness to his wife and honoring behavior toward her and other women.

6. Not a Recent Convert

Mature in their faith.

7. Proven Manager of Home and Family

If children are not following the Lord, it may not be the right time for them to take on the responsibility of the position of elder.

8. Appointment

   A process is important so you can tell what a person is really like.

III. TITUS AND 2 TIMOTHY

Titus was a pastor in Crete. 2 Timothy was primarily written as a personal letter to his friend Timothy to encourage him to persevere.

Questions

1. In the pastoral epistles, Paul closely connects sinful behavior with false teaching. Reflect on why one might influence the other. Is this a connection you have observed?

2. One of the instructions Paul gives to men specifically is that they should not be fighting in the middle of worship service. What are the things that cause the majority of disagreement and "fighting" in the church today (whether men or women)? Is this affecting worship service? What would Paul's advice be?

3. In the Pastorals, Paul instructs that women should not be dressing in ways that attract attention to themselves, especially sexual attention and attention because of their wealth. What are modern day parallels to this (for both men and women)? What can we encourage ourselves and others to do instead?

4. Reflect on the teaching on 1 Timothy 2:11-15 regarding women teaching. What is your background on this issue and what is your interpretation of this passage? How does this passage affect you personally?

5. The issue of women in leadership is a very difficult one today. Why does the conversation often get heated? What are ways to dialogue about this issue lovingly?

6. Of those who believe and teach false things, Paul says protect yourself: "Keep a close watch on yourself and on the teaching." Do you notice that you are negatively affected in character or beliefs by anyone around you? What should you do, according to these letters?

7. One of the main issues Paul addresses in the pastorals correcting others in error, but he is specific that this should be done with gentleness, saying that we "must not be quarrelsome, but kind to everyone, able to teach, patiently enduring evil, correcting his opponents with gentleness." That's really difficult. Are there specific situations where you need to heed this advice?

8. Recount a time when you have heard something taught that was false, and evaluate whether it was handled the way that Paul instructs in the Pastoral Epistles.

9. Is being an elder in a church something you aspire to? If so, identify where you are qualified and where growth is needed. If not, reflect on what you view as your role in your local church.

10. Identify the three main issues addressed in the pastoral epistles. Are these issues that our churches today need to continue to deal with? Are there a different "three main issues" that Paul would address if he wrote to your pastor today?

26

Hebrews

I. **INTRODUCTION**

   A. **Resources and Nature**

      NIV Application Commentary Series by George Guthrie, Eerdmans – Epistle to the Hebrews by F. F. Bruce. Part of the group known as general epistles.

   B. **Authorship, Date, and Recipients**

      The author is not named. It was likely written before a.d. 70. It was written to Jewish Christians.

C. Themes

Supremacy of Christ over all things, warning passages that emphasize the importance of perseverance.

D. Structural Overview

Supremacy of Christ over angels, supremacy of Christ over Moses, supremacy of Christ over the Jewish sacrificial system, and wome warning passages interspersed.

II. SUPREMACY OF CHRIST (HEB. 1:1-3)

Eight basic truths about Jesus

III. SUPREMACY OVER ANGELS (HEB. 1:4-2:18)

Some elements of Judaism worshipped angels

A. A Series of Old Testament Quotations

Psalm 2:7, 2 Samuel 7:14, Psalm 45

B. Warning #1 (Heb. 2:1-4)

Do not drift away from the truth about who Jesus is and what he has done to provide salvation.

C. Continues with Jesus's Supremacy (Heb. 2:5-18)

Jesus became human to free us from slavery to sin, and now is crowned with glory and honor.

D. Exposition #1: Call to Be Faithful (Hebrews 3-4)

The author of Hebrews writes like a pastor because he teaches you theology then stops occasionally to encourage people to be faithful.

IV. A POSITIVE AND NEGATIVE EXAMPLE OF FAITH (HEB. 3:1-19)

Compares the faithfulness of Jesus to the unfaithfulness of the Jews.

V. BE FAITHFUL TO ENTER THE REST (HEB. 4:1-13)

God promised that the Jews could enter into rest but they didn't.

VI. THE SUPERIORITY OF CHRIST TO THE JEWISH SACRIFICIAL SYSTEM (HEB. 4:14-10:18)

Christ's sacrifice accomplished salvation for all but Jewish sacrifices on their own did not accomplish anything.

A. Transition (Heb. 4:14-16)

The author was exhorting people to be faithful then began talking about Jesus as the high priest.

B. Jesus as the High Priest (Heb. 5:1-10)

1. Background: High Priests and Melchizedek

The priests in the Old Testament came from the tribe of Levi. The Bible does not give the genealogy for Melchizedek.

2. Jesus as the Superior High Priest

Jesus was not from the tribe of Levi, he was appointed by God like Melchizedek.

C. Warning #2 (Heb. 5:11-6:20)

   1. Encouragement toward Spiritual Maturity

      You ought to be teachers, but you need someone to teach you again the basic principles of the oracles of God.

   2. The Danger of Apostasy

      It is impossible to restore again to repentance those who have once been enlightened…

   3. The Arminian and Calvinist Debate

      Arminians say that you can lose your salvation. Calvinists say that you can't.

4. The Real Problem

Is it possible for someone who experienced a relationship with Christ to abandone him then come back?

5. Encouragement (Heb. 6:9-20)

God is going to be true to his commitment and true to his promise to you, so hang in there.

D. Superiority of Melchizedek (Hebrews 7)

Melchizedek was superior in his priesthood over that of Aaron and Jesus is a priest like Melchizedek, so Jesus is superior to the Jewish sacrificial system.

E. Superiority of Jesus's New Covenant (Heb. 8:1-10:18)

   1. The New Covenant Makes the Old Obsolete (Heb. 8:7-13)

       Jeremiah 31 describes the new covenant as a new way that God relates to his creation. It will be written on the heart, not on tablets of stone.

VII. EXPOSITION #2: THE ASSURANCE OF OUR FAITH (HEB. 10:19-11:40)

Chapter 10 warns you that if you go on sinning deliberately after receiving the knowledge of truth, there no longer remains a sacrifice for sins, but a fearful expectation of judgment. Chapter 11 gives a definition of faith and reflects on people of faith throughout history.

VIII. ETHICAL INSTRUCTIONS (HEB. 12:1-13:19)

Since we are surrounded by a great cloud of witnesses, let us run with endurance the race set before us, looking to Jesus who endured the cross and is seated at the right hand of God.

IX. CONCLUSION (13:22-25)

Hebrews 13:20, "Now may the God of peace who brought again from the dead our Lord Jesus, the great shepherd of the sheep, by the blood of the eternal covenant, equip you with everything good that you may do his will, working in us that which is pleasing in his sight, through Jesus Christ, to whom be glory forever and ever. Amen." That's his summation of the entire book and again you have this really neat idea that God equips us and it is his energy that allows us to do what is pleasing in his sight.

Questions

1. The author of Hebrews says that Jesus also experienced as a human being what you and I experience, and that in this way, he can serve as our high priest. Do you think of Jesus in this way—as a human, experiencing the things that we do? How does the doctrine of his humanity influence your faith?

2. In Heb. 5:11-6:20, the author warns not to give up and turn away, because if you do you're not coming back. Do you know of any stories of people experiencing Jesus or the church community, and then turning away? Did this make it more difficult for them to return, in your opinion? How does your experience relate to what the author is saying?

3. How can we hold in balance the warnings of the Book of Hebrews not to fall away and the assurance that God has made a commitment to us and perseveres on our behalf? Do you tend to hang on to one of these truths more than the other? Is it important to hold both equally?

4. In Hebrews 11, the audience is encouraged to be faithful in light of the many faithful believers who have gone before them. Are there particular faithful believers that encourage you? In what way?

5. Are there any truths from the Book of Hebrews that would be particularly effective in helping a Jewish person today see who Jesus is? Give one example, or explain your answer.

6. What is the situation that the author of Hebrews is addressing? Are there any modern day equivalents? How would you address these today?

7. How would you respond to someone who says that Jesus was just a good man or a prophet? What are some passages you could show them? What does the Book of Hebrews specifically contribute?

8. Read Hebrews 2:14-18. The evangelical church in America is more concerned with Jesus's divinity, rather than his humanity, but this is one of those really strong verses on his humanity. How could some of these truths be incorporated into our church or personal lives?

9. Make a list of the similarities and differences between Jesus the high priest and the sacrificial system of the Hebrew Bible. Then, answer the question: was there forgiveness in the Old Testament? Support your answer.

10. The author of Hebrews gives strong warnings against apostasy. What, in your opinion, are the strongest arguments for and against the possibility of Christians losing their salvation?

27

James

I. INTRODUCTION

A. Author and Date

The author is James, the brother of Jesus and also the head of the church in Jerusalem. It was probably written between a.d. 40-50.

B. Theme, Structure, and Resources

The theological theme is sanctification. A good commentary is NIVAC by David Nystrom.

II. JUSTIFICATION BY WORKS

A. Contradiction with Paul

Some of the statements in James about faith and works seem to contradict statements in Paul's letters.

B. Be Doers, Not Only Hearers (James 1:19-27)

The purpose of God's Word is for us to hear it and then do it.

C. Solution: "Justification" Has a Range of Meaning

All words have a range of meaning and the one that applies in any situation depends on the context.

D. Consequences of Hearing but Not Doing

Faith that doesn't have works cannot save.

III. PAIN AND SUFFERING

It's important to distinguish pain caused by living in a fallen world and pain caused by persecution. God can redeem pain you experience by helping you mature in your faith.

A. You will Meet Trials

Everyone experiences trials. If you are experiencing a trial it's not necessarily the result of sin you committed.

B. Respond in Joy Because of What the Trials Do

Respond in joy as you are experiencing trials because we can mature spiritually in the process.

C. The Goal

The goal is that we become more like Jesus.

D. Other Passages

Romans 5:1-5 has the same theme of persevering in suffering can produce character and hope. The problem of pain is a significant question: How can a good and powerful God allow suffering?

E. Resources

A Grace Disguised by Jerry Sittser, Misty Our Momentary Child by Carol Gift Page, When God Interrupts by Craig Barnes, The Problem of Pain by C. S. Lewis

IV. WHAT IS JUSTICE?

Justice must be defined by what God does. Our perspective as humans is limited, so by our standards, some of the things God does or allows seem unjust.

V. TEMPTATION AND SIN

Blessed is the man who remains steadfast under trial, for when he has stood the test he will receive the crown of life, which God has promised to those who love him. Let no one say when he is tempted, "I am being tempted by God," for God cannot be tempted with evil and he himself tempts no one. But each person is tempted when he is lured and enticed by his own desire. Then desire when it has conceived gives birth to sin, and sin when it is fully grown brings forth death. (James 1:12-15)

A. The Necessity of Persevering Under Temptation

When you stand the test and persevere, you will receive the crown of life.

B. The Source of Temptation

The source of temptation is not God.

C. Our Own Desires (James 1:14)

We are tempted to sin because our desires pull us and our passions push us.

D. Friendship with the World (James 4:1-4)

Whoever wishes to be a friend of the world makes himself to be an enemy of God.

E. Solutions to Sin and Temptation

There is a promised blessing if you resist and endure temptation. Don't be friends with the world. There is a battle going on inside of us. God is on our side. Humble yourself and draw near to God.

Temptation is not sin. It's how you choose to respond to temptation that determines if you sin or not.

VI. THE TONGUE

A. James 1:26

If anyone thinks he is religious and does not bridle his tongue, but deceives his heart, this person's religion is worthless.

B. James 3:1-12

The tongue is powerful. The consequences of what you say can be destructive.

C. How Can the Tongue Be So Powerful?

What you say shows who you really are. Comments that you make to others and about others can be encouraging or destructive.

VII. ADDITIONAL TOPICS: IMMUTABILITY, WEALTH, AND PRAYER

Prayer is powerful. God does not change. You should not accumulate wealth by oppressing others.

Questions

1. What is your experience with the health and wealth Gospel that teaches that all suffering is due to sin? Have you heard this preached? Do you subconsciously think this way?

2. Reflect on James's call to respond with joy in times of trial, because we know that the trials are producing steadfastness and Christian maturity. It may be helpful to think about how an Olympic athlete endures phenomenal pain to achieve the goal and our goal is Christian maturity. Have you ever experienced joy in the midst of a trial? If not, what would this look like in the future?

3. In Roman Catholic theology, works, whether your own deeds or the merits of the saints, play a strong role in justification. Is this different than what James says?

4. What is your view of temptation—is it sin? Always? Sometimes? Never? The lecture addressed solutions to sin and temptation. Which did you find most helpful, and why?

5. Why does James say the tongue is so powerful? What does your tongue reveal about you? Do you identify with any of the reasons for letting the tongue loose in the lecture?

6. James 1:27 says, "Religion that is pure and undefiled before God, the Father, is this: to visit orphans and widows in their affliction, and to keep oneself unstained from the world." Reflect on how the church typically understands religion, and come up with some practical ways to live out "true religion" in your own life or church community.

7. What is the apparent contradiction between Paul and James? How could you explain to a new believer that there is a solution to this contradiction?

8. The book of James highlights that changed people live in changed ways, and that faith without works is dead. Reflect on the connection between faith and works in your own life. How does God want you to respond to this message in James? Be specific and concrete.

9. Reading James brings up questions about whether people we know are truly saved, since even though they profess to be Christians, their works to not match up. It was argued in the lecture that rather than trying to figure out if someone is truly a Christian, we should do something about it. Do you know any such people? What is God calling you to do, specifically?

10. If someone asked you why the immutability of God mattered, what would you say?

28

Peter and Jude

I. 1 PETER

A. Introduction

1. Authorship and Date

Written in the 60's by the apostle Peter, possibly with the help of a secretary.

2. Themes

Encouragement to persevere and be faithful when you are experiencing suffering as a result of your faith. Look forward to the return of Jesus in the future.

B. **Salutation (1 Pet. 1:1-2)**

If you are a believer, you are temporarily in the world but your citizenship is in heaven.

C. **Basic Idea Summarized (1 Pet. 1:3-9)**

We are exiles because God has caused us to be born again. We have a living hope, we have an inheritance, and we must live out our lives in holiness and obedience.

D. **Fact of Suffering (1 Pet. 1:6-7)**

Sometimes you suffer because you live in a sinful world and sometimes because someone persecutes you because of your faith.

1. **Perspective: Suffering is Only for a "Little While"**

    Suffering is painful when you are experiencing it, but it is only for a short time when you compare it to eternity.

2. **Remember What Suffering Accomplishes**

    When you persevere, God commends you, it produces character and hope and you become more like Christ.

3. **Present Faithfulness and Future Orientation Combined**

    We love God even though we haven't seen him and as a result, God has saved us.

4. Motivations for Godly Living

You should be like Jesus, God judges impartially based on your deeds, Jesus paid a high cost to redeem you.

E. Other Themes in 1 Peter

1. The Priesthood of All Believers

God invites us directly into his presence.

2. Be Prepared to Make a Defense

When people ask you about the hope that you have in God, be ready to explain it to them.

II. 2 PETER

A. Authorship

1. Written by the Apostle Peter

2. The Relationship Between 2 Peter and Jude

Both deal with a situation involving false teachers, so it's likely that Jude used what was relevant from 2 Peter as part of his letter.

B. Important Verses in 2 Peter

1. 2 Peter 1:20-21

"No prophecy of Scripture comes from someone's own interpretation. For no prophecy was ever produced by the will of man, but men spoke from God as they were carried along by the Holy Spirit." Also 2 Peter 3:16 and 2 Peter 3:8.

III. JUDE

   A. Introduction

   Probably a brother of Jesus. Written in the late 60's.

   B. Historical Situation (Jude 3-4)

      1. "Contend"

         Jude is calling his audience to fight aggressively for the faith.

      2. "Faith"

         Faith refers to our personal faith in Jesus, and also to describe the set of core beliefs that define who we are as believers.

3. **"Once for All Delivered to The Saints"**

   By the time Jude was written, the basic teaching of who Jesus is and what it means to be a disciple of Jesus is set.

4. **"Certain People Have Snuck in"**

   The false teachers became leaders in the church. They were devoid of the Spirit.

C. Description, Condemnation, and Solution to False Teachers (Jude 5-23)

You must be faithful in your walk with God, because if you turn away, you will be punished.

1. **Don't Be Surprised (Jude 17-19)**

   No matter how well your church seems to be doing, don't be surprised with ungodly people come in and try to cause divisions.

2. Devote Yourself to Your Own Spiritual Growth (Jude 20-21)

You need to be growing spiritually so that you can deal with false teachers when they come.

3. Fight for The Faith (Jude 22-23)

Be ready to deal with people who are doubting their faith, those who might be almost convinced to follow false teaching, and the false teachers themselves.

D. Doxology (24-25)

The power to deal with false teachers and the situations they cause comes from, "…him who is able to keep you from stumbling."

Questions

1. What joy or reassurance do you find in 1 Pet. 1:3-5?

2. Read the challenge in 1 Peter 1:15-16. What does the word "holy" mean? From what passage is Peter quoting in verse 16? Is it a reasonable command? Why or why not? How can you apply it to your life?

3. In 1 Peter, Peter consistently calls his readers to not only live in the present, but also to look to our future hope. The counter to 1 Peter is the human tendency to look down at your feet and not see anything beyond them. How does this call impact your own life?

4. In 1 Peter, Peter offers various motivations for enduring suffering. Identify some of these and which you find most motivating.

5. What are the two core doctrines that Jude says Christians must stand up and fight for? Why are these doctrines so important? One of Jude's solutions to dealing with false teachers is to be devoted to our own spiritual growth. Do you hold these two core doctrines in high regard in your own life? How can you do so even more?

6. In 1 Pet. 1:17, what do you think Peter means when he tells us to "conduct yourselves in fear"? What clues does the context give?

7. Compare the idea of biblical hope, confident assurance, with other understandings of hope.

8. In 1 Pet. 2:2-9, what is the meaning of Christ as a cornerstone, and as ourselves as living stones? What event in Peter's life might have inspired this metaphor?

9. Why is the priesthood of all believers significant (1 Pet. 2:9)? What do priests do? What should you do, in light of this?

10. Imagine talking to someone who believes that it was only in church councils in later centuries that the Scriptural canon was developed, and therefore they may have gotten it wrong. What do 2 Pet. 3:16 and Jude 3 each contribute to the discussion?

29

John's Letters

I. INTRODUCTION TO JOHN'S LETTERS

A. Author and Date

Written in the late first century by the Apostle John that also wrote the Gospel of John.

B. False Teaching of Pre-Gnosticism

A belief in dualism which teaches that there are the two separate realms of the material and the spiritual. Material is evil and spiritual is good. Their goal is to leave the material world and move into a spiritual existence.

C. John's Answer to Gnosticism

Jesus is fully human as well as God, it's important to love your brother, as we live out our lives and grow in love and obedience, we have assurance that we are in relationship with God.

II. 1 JOHN

A. John Asserts His Authority (1 John 1:1-4)

John is writing this letter based on his relationship to God and his personal experience of physically being with Jesus.

B. Role of On-Going Sin in the Life of the Believer (1 John 1:5-2:6)

The message of the false teachers was to sin all you want and God will forgive you.

1. **Biblical Dualism**

    If we say we have fellowship with him while we walk in the darkness, we lie. If we walk in the light as he is in the light, we have fellowship with one another and the blood of Jesus his Son cleanses us from all sin.

2. **The Exegetical Issue of Strong Language**

    John pictures the world as black and white to make an important point about the false teachers, but he also admits there is gray.

3. **Assurance (1 John 2:1-6)**

    a) **Assurance is Based in Forgiveness (1 John 2:1-2)**

    Part of your assurance that you are a Christian is that when you do sin, you will be forgiven if you ask.

b) Assurance is Contained in Our Obedience (1 John 2:3-6)

If you are in relationship with God, the way you live will change.

c) Assurance Through the Inner Witness of the Holy Spirit

Part of the function of the Holy Spirit is that he is in our lives and subjectively internally confirming that we are his children.

d) True Belief

There is a direct relationship between salvation and sanctification.

4. Command to Love (1 John 2:7-17)

   a) The Same Commandment that Jesus Taught

   Jesus commanded us to love one another.

   b) Love versus Hate of a Brother

   It matters how we relate to each other.

   c) What is Love?

   As you look at the effects of God's love, you can come to a better understanding of what love is.

   d) Loving God versus Loving the World

   What you think about, how you spend your money and how you use your time are indications of what you think is important.

5. Antichrists (1 John 2:18-27)

   a) Lack of Perseverance Shows They Are Not Christians

   Since they left, they may not have been believers in the first place.

   b) They Deny the Reality of the Incarnation

   Jesus was both fully God and fully human.

Questions

1. One of the primary things John is confronting in 1 John is the idea that it doesn't matter how we live our lives, and that we can sin all we want and God will forgive us. What are the primary reasons that drive people to think this way? Do you tend to fall into any of these traps? What are the best ways to convince and motivate someone (ourselves and others) that it does matter?

2. John speaks in very black and white terms about love and hate of others. It doesn't seem that he wants us to figure out where the line is between love and hate to see if we can "dislike" but not hate someone. Rather, John wants us to exemplify the love of God in our lives, that we would lay down our lives for others. Is there a specific person (think especially of whether there is someone that you tend to dislike) that you need to show this kind of love to? Come up with an action plan.

3. John warns of false teachers. What kinds of things do you have in place in your life to minimize the chances of being led astray?

4. John is very blunt in 1 John 2:15, making it clear that we cannot love the world and God. What does it mean to love the world? Why would believers choose to love the world more than God? How can we resist this?

5. What does it mean that God is love? (1 John 4:8) Is it equally true that love is God? Explain.

6. What are the primary markers of Gnosticism talked about in the lecture? Can you identify any modern-day examples of this kind of belief?

7. What is the relationship between becoming saved and living saved, between salvation and sanctification? Would you incorporate both into your sharing of the Gospel? Why or why not, and what would that look like?

8. 1 John 1:8-9 is an incredible truth: "8If we say we have no sin, we deceive ourselves, and the truth is not in us. 9But if we confess our sins, he is faithful and just to forgive us our sins and to cleanse us from all unrighteousness." Meditate on this truth, and spend some time confessing your sin to God and believing that he cleanses and forgives you.

9. How is love defined in 1 John? What are other definitions of love set forward in the world? How does John's definition challenge your own life—be concrete and specific.

10. Imagine you are talking to someone who believes that their sin is far too great for God to forgive. How would you minister to this person, especially from 1 John?

30

Revelation

I. **INTRODUCTION**

    A. **Resources**

        New International Commentary on the New Testament by Robert Mounce, What are We Waiting For by Robert Mounce, Breaking the Code to Understanding the Book of Revelation by Bruce Metzger

    B. **Author and Date**

        Written in the mid 90's by the Apostle John

C. Apocalyptic Genre

Apocalyptic literature deals with the end times using symbolic language. A common theme is the fight of good versus evil.

D. Three Key Questions for Interpretation

1. Symbolism: Metaphorical or Literal?

The pictures that John paints in the Book of Revelation are symbols, but they are symbols of real things.

2. Relationship of the Three Cycles: Linear or Cyclical?

It's possible that John is using all three cycles as a description of the same series of events because at the end of each of them it sounds like final judgment.

3. What is the Central Theme?

It's going to get worse, God is going to win, so be faithful.

II. LETTERS TO THE CHURCHES (REV. 2:1-3:7)

These are real churches and God has an individual message for each one.

A. Vision of the Future

Revelation is not specific about the time frame referred to by, "After this," in 4:1.

1. Preterism

All the events in the book of Revelation, including the return of Jesus, were fulfilled by a.d. 70 when the Roman army destroyed the temple in Jerusalem

2. Church Historical School

The events in 4:2 up to the time of Christ refer to historical events stretching over a 2,000 year period.

3. Futurism

There is a huge time gap between the end of chapter 3 and the beginning of chapter 4 and everything is in the future. Dispensationalists fit in this group.

4. Middle Position

Most of the prophecies were fulfilled by a.d. 70, but prophecies often have multiple fulfillments that go in cycles. There will be an ultimate fulfillment with an Antichrist that is worse than anything we have seen. Events will grow in intensity and there will be an end of time.

III. THRONE ROOM SCENE (REV. 4-5)

The imagery is meant to describe the holiness, grandeur, majesty and power and everything that is God's.

IV. CYCLE #1: SEVEN SEALS AND INTERLUDE (REV. 6-7)

The scroll can't be opened until all seven seals are broken. At the end you have judgment, God's salvation and people living with God with the Lamb in their midst.

V. CYCLE #2: SEVEN TRUMPETS AND INTERLUDE (REV. 8-11)

Six trumpets sound, there is an interlude, then the seventh trumpet sounds and there is judgment.

VI. THE DRAGON AND THE TWO BEASTS (REV. 12-14)

A. The Birth of Jesus (Rev. 12:1-6)

Jesus is born, Satan tries to destroy him, but Jesus is caught up to God and his throne.

B. Michael and the Dragon (Rev. 12:7-17)

Satan's defeat was before Adam and Eve. John is doing the best he can to record the vision he is experiencing.

C. The First Beast from the Seas (Rev. 13:1-10)

John wants to encourage believers to persevere even though the beast looks frightening.

D. The Second Beast (The False Prophet) (Rev. 13:1-10)

Revelation describes the Antichrist as a human being that had a mortal wound but did not die, and will likely claim to be God. Satan will work miracles through him.

VII. THE VIEW FROM HEAVEN (REV. 14)

A call for endurance of the saints and an encouragement to be faithful even though you are experiencing persecution.

VIII. CYCLE #3: SEVEN BOWLS AND JUDGMENT (REV. 15-28)

The third cycle of seven. Even after these events, people don't repent.

IX. FINAL VICTORY (REV. 19:1-20:10)

A. Hallelujah, Marriage, and Judgment (Rev. 19)

Marriage supper of the marriage between the bride, which is all believers, and the Lamb, which is Jesus. Also you have the judgment of other people.

B. The Millennium (Rev. 20:1-10)

Three positions to explain the period of the millennium are post-millennialism, pre-millenialism and amillennialism.

X. **FINAL JUDGMENT AND HEAVEN (REV. 20:11-22:5)**

   Creation of the new heaven and new earth, and people are judged by whether or not their names are in the book of life.

Questions

1. What do you think about calling faithfulness to the point of martyrdom a "conquering?" What does the imagery convey to you in a positive sense?

2. How would you feel if an apostle wrote your church a letter and congratulated on what you were doing right, critiqued you on what you were doing wrong, and then called you to faithfulness to the point of death, if necessary? How different would your church service be? Would it be a good or bad difference?

3. The idea of Satan being defeated but still powerful is, I think, a difficult concept. He seems so powerful to us today. How have you seen Satan to be powerful but defeated? How is this an encouragement?

4. Do you think about yourself much as the bride of Christ and that someday you will celebrate the marriage feast of the lamb? Reflect on this.

5. Share what you think heaven is going to be like. Gold? A garden? Restored earth?

6. Identify all the markers you can of the apocalyptic genre and all of the books in the New Testament that use this genre. Discuss the problems with being overly literal or over symbolic. Do you think John expects us to understand the details symbolically?

7. How do you feel about the approach that sees the three cycles of seven as cyclical? Or do you think they are sequential? Support your answer.

8. What do you think is the central theme of the book? How would you teach the book to people—both children and adults—so that the central theme stays central?

9. Because both the beast and the false prophet will do miracles, it is imperative that we do not automatically believe any wonder-worker that comes our way? How will you protect yourself?

10. In what way is eschatology ethical in the book of Revelation? How does eschatology encourage you to be faithful? Please be practical in your application.

31

Annotated Statement of Faith

I. ARTICLE ONE: SCRIPTURE

The Bible is the infallible word of God, the supreme rule for faith and practice.[1]

The sixty-six books of the Old and New Testament[2] came

---

1   Infallibility – Every word of God proves true; he is a shield to those who take refuge in him (Prov 30:5). Your word is truth (John 17:17). Scripture cannot be broken (John 10:35). For truly, I say to you, until heaven and earth pass away, not an iota, not a dot, will pass from the Law until all is accomplished (Matt 5:18). The promises were spoken to Abraham and to his seed. The Scripture does not say "and to seeds," meaning many people, but "and to your seed," meaning one person, who is Christ (Gal 3:16). And we impart this in words not taught by human wisdom but taught by the Spirit, interpreting spiritual truths to those who are spiritual (1 Cor 2:13). But the Helper, the Holy Spirit, whom the Father will send in my name, he will teach you all things and bring to your remembrance all that I have said to you (John 14:26). When the Spirit of truth comes, he will guide you into all the truth, for he will not speak on his own authority, but whatever he hears he will speak, and he will declare to you the things that are to come. He will glorify me, for he will take what is mine and declare it to you (John 16:13-14).

2   Canonicity – There are some things in them that are hard to understand, which the ignorant and unstable twist to their own destruction, as they do the other Scriptures (2 Pet 3:16). Beloved, although I was very eager to write to you about our common salvation, I found it necessary to write appealing to you to contend for the faith that was once for all delivered to the saints (Jude 1:3). I warn everyone who hears the words of the prophecy of this

from the very mouth of God[3] and are without error in the originals, faithfully preserved through the centuries. Scripture is therefore the unique and supreme guide for all it affirms, including both belief and behavior.[4]

The teachings of the Bible are sufficient for salvation and sanctification.[5] While there are questions of meaning and application over which we may agree to disagree, there is nothing for which we are responsible to God in terms of our salvation and sanctification that is not expressed in Scripture, either in precept or principle.

From these convictions flow the following articles of faith.

---

book: if anyone adds to them, God will add to him the plagues described in this book, and if anyone takes away from the words of the book of this prophecy, God will take away his share in the tree of life and in the holy city, which are described in this book (Rev 22:18-19).

3   Inspiration – Lectures 1-2 – All Scripture is breathed out by God and profitable for teaching, for reproof, for correction, and for training in righteousness, that the man of God may be competent, equipped for every good work (2 Tim 3:16-17). For no prophecy was ever produced by the will of man, but men spoke from God as they were carried along by the Holy Spirit (2 Pet 1:21).

4   Plenary inspiration – All Scripture is breathed out by God (2 Tim 3:16). For the word of God is living and active, sharper than any two-edged sword, piercing to the division of soul and of spirit, of joints and of marrow, and discerning the thoughts and intentions of the heart. And no creature is hidden from his sight, but all are naked and exposed to the eyes of him to whom we must give account (Heb 4:12-13).

5   Sufficiency of Scripture – All Scripture is breathed out by God and profitable for teaching, for reproof, for correction, and for training in righteousness, that the man of God may be competent, equipped for every good work (2 Tim 3:16-17).

II. ARTICLE TWO: TRINITY

There is one God,[1] infinitely perfect,[2] without change,[3] creator of all yet not created,[4] distinct from His creation yet everywhere present,[5] perfectly balanced in all His attributes,[6] omniscient over all time,[7] wholly sovereign.[8] He alone is the

---

1 Monotheism – Hear, O Israel: The LORD our God, the LORD is one (Deut 6:4). You shall not make for yourself a carved image, or any likeness of anything that is in heaven above, or that is in the earth beneath, or that is in the water under the earth (Exod 20:4). For there is one God, and there is one mediator between God and men, the man Christ Jesus (1 Tim 2:5).

2 Perfection –

3 Immutability – The Father of lights with whom there is no variation or shadow due to change (James 1:17). Jesus Christ is the same yesterday and today and forever (Heb 13:8). Of old you laid the foundation of the earth, and the heavens are the work of your hands. They will perish, but you will remain; they will all wear out like a garment. You will change them like a robe, and they will pass away, but you are the same, and your years have no end (Ps 102:25-27).

4 Creation – All things were made through him, and without him was not anything made that was made (John 1:3). For by him all things were created, in heaven and on earth, visible and invisible, whether thrones or dominions or rulers or authorities – all things were created through him and for him (Col 1:16).

5 Omnipresence –

6

7 Omniscience –

8 Sovereignty – For I am God, and there is no other; I am God, and there is none like me, declaring the end from the beginning and from ancient times things not yet done, saying, "My counsel shall stand, and I will accomplish all my purpose" (Isa 46:9-10). I know that you can do all things, and that no purpose of yours can be thwarted (Job 42:2). Our God is in the heavens; he does all that he pleases (Ps 115:3). And we know that for those who love God all things work together for good, for those who are called according to his purpose. For those whom he foreknew he also predestined to be conformed to the image of his Son, in order that he might be the firstborn among many brothers Rom 8:28-29). In him we have obtained an inheritance, having been predestined according to the purpose of him who works all things according to the counsel of his will (Eph 1:11).

sole object of worship.[9]

God exists eternally in three persons—Father, Son, Holy Spirit—equal in essence and divine perfection, all three uncreated, executing distinct but harmonious offices.[10]

III. ARTICLE THREE: GOD THE FATHER

God the Father is an infinite, personal spirit, perfect in holiness, wisdom, power and love. He concerns himself mercifully in the affairs of his creation, hearing and answering prayers, saving from sin all who come to him through Jesus Christ. All life is to be lived ultimately for his glory.

---

9 Worship – You shall have no other gods before me. You shall not make for yourself a carved image, or any likeness of anything that is in heaven above, or that is in the earth beneath, or that is in the water under the earth. You shall not bow down to them or serve them, for I the LORD your God am a jealous God, visiting the iniquity of the fathers on the children to the third and the fourth generation of those who hate me, but showing steadfast love to thousands of those who love me and keep my commandments (Exod 20:3-6).

10 Trinity – Go therefore and make disciples of all nations, baptizing them in the name of the Father and of the Son and of the Holy Spirit (Matt 28:19). The grace of the Lord Jesus Christ and the love of God and the fellowship of the Holy Spirit be with you all (2 Cor 13:14). Eph 1:3-14.

IV. ARTICLE FOUR: GOD THE SON

God the Son is fully God[1] and fully human,[2] without confusion

---

1   Divinity – John 1:1-19, 34; 10:30; Mark 1:1; 2:10; Col 1:15-20 – These are written so that you may believe that Jesus is the Christ, the Son of God, and that by believing you may have life in his name (John 20:31). In the beginning was the Word, and the Word was with God, and the Word was God. He was in the beginning with God. All things were made through him, and without him was not anything made that was made (John 1:1-3). No one has ever seen God; the only God, who is at the Father's side, he has made him known (John 1:18). This was why the Jews were seeking all the more to kill him, because not only was he breaking the Sabbath, but he was even calling God his own Father, making himself equal with God (John 5:18). Jesus said to him, "Have I been with you so long, and you still do not know me, Philip? Whoever has seen me has seen the Father. How can you say, "Show us the Father"? (John 14:9). Behold, the virgin shall conceive and bear a son, and they shall call his name "Immanuel" (which means, God with us) (Matt 1:23). No one knows the Son except the Father, and no one knows the Father except the Son and anyone to whom the Son chooses to reveal him (Matt 11:27). I and the Father are one (John 10:30). Whoever sees me sees him who sent me (John 12:45). To them belong the patriarchs, and from their race, according to the flesh, is the Christ who is God over all, blessed forever. Amen (Rom 9:5). He is the image of the invisible God, the firstborn of all creation (Col 1:15). For in him the whole fullness of deity dwells bodily (Col 2:9). Waiting for our blessed hope, the appearing of the glory of our great God and Savior Jesus Christ (Titus 2:13). He is the radiance of the glory of God and the exact imprint of his nature, and he upholds the universe by the word of his power (Heb 1:3). But of the Son he says, "Your throne, O God, is forever and ever, the scepter of uprightness is the scepter of your kingdom" (Heb 1:8). Simeon Peter, a servant and apostle of Jesus Christ, to those who have obtained a faith of equal standing with ours by the righteousness of our God and Savior Jesus Christ (2 Pet 1:1). I am the Alpha and the Omega, the first and the last, the beginning and the end (Rev 22:13).

2   Humanity, Incarnation – Matt 1:18-25; John 1:14 – And the Word became flesh and dwelt among us, and we have seen his glory, glory as of the only Son from the Father, full of grace and truth (John 1:14). And the angel answered her, "The Holy Spirit will come upon you, and the power of the Most High will overshadow you; therefore the child to be born will be called holy – the Son of God" (Luke 1:35). For our sake he made him to be sin who knew no sin, so that in him we might become the righteousness of God (2 Cor 5:21). But when Christ had offered for all time a single sacrifice for sins, he sat down at the right hand of God, waiting from that time until his enemies should be made a footstool for his feet. For by a single offering he has perfected for all time those who are being sanctified (Heb 10:12-14). For the Lord himself will descend from heaven with a cry of command, with the

or mixture, the unique and only Son.[3] He existed before time,[4] was conceived by the Holy Spirit,[5] born of the virgin Mary,[6] lived a sinless life,[7] died on the cross as the sacrifice for our sins,[8] was physically raised from the dead as prophesied,[9] ascended into heaven,[10] and is now exalted,[11] sitting at the right hand of God the Father, interceding for the saints as the sole

---

voice of an archangel, and with the sound of the trumpet of God (1 Thess 4:16). Therefore God has highly exalted him and bestowed on him the name that is above every name, so that at the name of Jesus every knee should bow, in heaven and on earth and under the earth, and every tongue confess that Jesus Christ is Lord, to the glory of God the Father (Phil 2:9-11). By this you know the Spirit of God: every spirit that confesses that Jesus Christ has come in the flesh is from God, and every spirit that does not confess Jesus is not from God. This is the spirit of the antichrist, which you heard was coming and now is in the world already (1 John 4:2-3).

3   Uniqueness – Mark 1:11 (Psalm 2:7); John 1:18 – You are my beloved Son; with you I am well pleased (Mark 1:11). No one has ever seen God; the only God, who is at the Father's side, he has made him known (John 1:18).

4   Pre-existence – In the beginning was the Word, and the Word was with God, and the Word was God (John 1:1).

5   Son of God – Matt 1:20-23.

6   Virgin birth – Matt 1:20-23.

7   Sinlessness – For we do not have a high priest who is unable to sympathize with our weaknesses, but one who in every respect has been tempted as we are, yet without sin (Heb 4:15). For God has done what the law, weakened by the flesh, could not do. By sending his own Son in the likeness of sinful flesh and for sin, he condemned sin in the flesh (Rom 8:3).

8   Atonement – For even the Son of Man came not to be served but to serve, and to give his life as a ransom for many (Mark 10:45).

9   Mark 16:1-8; kerygma (Acts 2:22-32).

10 Ascension – And when he had said these things, as they were looking on, he was lifted up, and a cloud took him out of their sight (Acts 1:9).

11 Exaltation – Therefore God has highly exalted him and bestowed on him the name that is above every name, so that at the name of Jesus every knee should bow, in heaven and on earth and under the earth, and every tongue confess that Jesus Christ is Lord, to the glory of God the Father (Phil 2:9-11). If you confess with your mouth that Jesus is Lord and believe in your heart that God raised him from the dead, you will be saved (Rom 10:9).

mediator.[1] He will return to earth,[2] and ultimately every knee shall bow and every tongue confess that Jesus Christ is Lord.[3]

V. ARTICLE FIVE: GOD THE HOLY SPIRIT

God the Spirit is sent to convict the world of sin, righteousness, and judgment.[4] He fully indwells every true believer[5] as a guarantee of his inheritance,[6] guides and empowers them,[7] gifts them for ministry,[8] interceding in

---

1   Intercession – For there is one God, and there is one mediator between God and men, the man Christ Jesus (1 Tim 2:5).

2   Return – see Article Ten: Eschatology

3   Lordship – Therefore God has highly exalted him and bestowed on him the name that is above every name, so that at the name of Jesus every knee should bow, in heaven and on earth and under the earth, and every tongue confess that Jesus Christ is Lord, to the glory of God the Father (Phil 2:9-11). If you confess with your mouth that Jesus is Lord and believe in your heart that God raised him from the dead, you will be saved (Rom 10:9).

4   But if I go, I will send him to you. And when he comes, he will convict the world concerning sin and righteousness and judgment: concerning sin, because they do not believe in me; concerning righteousness, because I go to the Father, and you will see me no longer; concerning judgment, because the ruler of this world is judged (John 16:7-11).

5   Indwelling – Being therefore exalted at the right hand of God, and having received from the Father the promise of the Holy Spirit, he has poured out this that you yourselves are seeing and hearing (Acts 2:33).

6   Guarantor – In him you also, when you heard the word of truth, the gospel of your salvation, and believed in him, were sealed with the promised Holy Spirit, who is the guarantee of our inheritance until we acquire possession of it, to the praise of his glory (Eph 1:13-14).

7   Guide –

8   1 Cor 12-14; Rom 12:3-8; Eph 4:11-12.

accordance with the will of God,[9] witnessing to Jesus.[10]

VI. ARTICLE SIX: ANTHROPOLOGY (DOCTRINE OF MAN)

Adam and Eve were both created in the image of God, Adam from the dust of the ground and Eve from his side.[11] They disobeyed God and died, spiritually and physically.[12] Therefore, all people are objects of wrath,[13] sinners by nature

---

9   Intercession – In the same way, the Spirit helps us in our weakness. We do not know what we ought to pray for, but the Spirit himself intercedes for us with groans that words cannot express. And he who searches our hearts knows the mind of the Spirit, because the Spirit intercedes for the saints in accordance with God's will (Rom 8:26-27).

10   But when the Helper comes, whom I will send to you from the Father, the Spirit of truth, who proceeds from the Father, he will bear witness about me (John 15:26).

11   Creation – So God created man in his own image, in the image of God he created him; male and female he created them (Gen 1:27). The LORD God formed the man of dust from the ground and breathed into his nostrils the breath of life, and the man became a living creature (Gen 2:7). So the LORD God caused a deep sleep to fall upon the man, and while he slept took one of his ribs and closed up its place with flesh. And the rib that the LORD God had taken from the man he made into a woman and brought her to the man (Gen 2:20-21).

12   Death – And the LORD God commanded the man, "You are free to eat from any tree in the garden; but you must not eat from the tree of the knowledge of good and evil, for when you eat of it you will surely die" (Gen 2:16-17). So when the woman saw that the tree was good for food, and that it was a delight to the eyes, and that the tree was to be desired to make one wise, she took of its fruit and ate, and she also gave some to her husband who was with her, and he ate (Gen 3:6).

13   Hamartiology – And you were dead in the trespasses and sins in which you once walked, following the course of this world, following the prince of the power of the air, the spirit that is now at work in the sons of disobedience—among whom we all once lived in the passions of our flesh, carrying out the desires of the body and the mind, and were by nature children of wrath, like the rest of mankind But God, being rich in mercy, because of the great love with which he loved us, even when we were dead in our trespasses, made us alive together with Christ—by grace you have been saved (Eph 2:1-3). For the wrath of God is revealed from heaven against all

and by choice.[1] They are dead in their sins and incapable of pleasing God.[2] Without the direct intervention of God, they will live separated from God, die in their sins, and receive the condemnation that their sin deserves.[3]

VII. ARTICLE SEVEN: SOTERIOLOGY (DOCTRINE OF SALVATION)

Salvation from sin and access to God is available only through

---

ungodliness and unrighteousness of men, who by their unrighteousness suppress the truth (Rom 1:18). What if God, desiring to show his wrath and to make known his power, has endured with much patience vessels of wrath prepared for destruction, in order to make known the riches of his glory for vessels of mercy, which he has prepared beforehand for glory (Rom 9:22-23).

1   Hamartiology – Rom 3:9-20 – If, because of one man's trespass, death reigned through that one man, much more will those who receive the abundance of grace and the free gift of righteousness reign in life through the one man Jesus Christ. Therefore, as one trespass led to condemnation for all men, so one act of righteousness leads to justification and life for all men. For as by the one man's disobedience the many were made sinners, so by the one man's obedience the many will be made righteous (Rom 5:17-19). For the wages of sin is death, but the free gift of God is eternal life in Christ Jesus our Lord (Rom 6:23). All have sinned and fall short of the glory of God (Rom 3:23). And you were dead in the trespasses and sins (Eph 2:1). God shows his love for us in that while we were still sinners, Christ died for us (Rom 5:8).

2   Those who are in the flesh cannot please God (Rom 8:8). And you were dead in the trespasses and sins in which you once walked, following the course of this world, following the prince of the power of the air, the spirit that is now at work in the sons of disobedience—among whom we all once lived in the passions of our flesh, carrying out the desires of the body and the mind, and were by nature children of wrath, like the rest of mankind (Eph 2:1-3).

3   Condemnation – For the wages of sin is death, but the free gift of God is eternal life in Christ Jesus our Lord (Rom 6:23). For those who live according to the flesh set their minds on the things of the flesh, but those who live according to the Spirit set their minds on the things of the Spirit. To set the mind on the flesh is death, but to set the mind on the Spirit is life and peace. For the mind that is set on the flesh is hostile to God, for it does not submit to God's law; indeed, it cannot. Those who are in the flesh cannot please God (Rom 8:5-8).

the work of Christ on the cross,[4] given by God's grace, mercy, and love,[5] received solely by faith[6] in Jesus Christ.[7] In conversion, the believer is drawn by God to Himself,[8]

---

4   Sufficiency of the Atonement – Mark 15:33-41; Isa 52:13-53:12 – "Behold, the Lamb of God, who takes away the sin of the world! (John 1:29). Jesus said to him, "I am the way, and the truth, and the life. No one comes to the Father except through me" (John 14:6). Christ redeemed us from the curse of the law by becoming a curse for us – for it is written, "Cursed is everyone who is hanged on a tree" (Gal 3:13). For our sake he made him to be sin who knew no sin, so that in him we might become the righteousness of God (2 Cor 5:21). In him we have redemption through his blood, the forgiveness of our trespasses, according to the riches of his grace (Eph 1:7). God shows his love for us in that while we were still sinners, Christ died for us (Rom 5:8).

5   God as Savior – Titus 2:11-14; 3:4-7 – But God, being rich in mercy, because of the great love with which he loved us, even when we were dead in our trespasses, made us alive together with Christ – by grace you have been saved– and raised us up with him and seated us with him in the heavenly places in Christ Jesus, so that in the coming ages he might show the immeasurable riches of his grace in kindness toward us in Christ Jesus. For by grace you have been saved through faith. And this is not your own doing; it is the gift of God, not a result of works, so that no one may boast (Eph 2:4-9).

6   Salvation by faith – Rom 3:21-25; Gal 2:15-4:7 – For by grace you have been saved through faith. And this is not your own doing; it is the gift of God, not a result of works, so that no one may boast (Eph 2:8-9). For I am not ashamed of the gospel, for it is the power of God for salvation to everyone who believes, to the Jew first and also to the Greek For in it the righteousness of God is revealed from faith for faith, as it is written, "The righteous shall live by faith" (Rom 1:16-17). Who saved us and called us to a holy calling, not because of our works but because of his own purpose and grace, which he gave us in Christ Jesus before the ages began (2 Tim 1:9). The righteousness of God through faith in Jesus Christ for all who believe. For there is no distinction: for all ... are justified by his grace as a gift, through the redemption that is in Christ Jesus (Rom 3:22,24). Blessed are the poor in spirit, for theirs is the kingdom of heaven. Blessed are those who mourn, for they shall be comforted. Blessed are the meek, for they shall inherit the earth. Blessed are those who hunger and thirst for righteousness, for they shall be satisfied (Matt 5:3-6). And without faith it is impossible to please him, for whoever would draw near to God must believe that he exists and that he rewards those who seek him (Heb 11:6). Also Rom 4; Heb 10:19-11:40.

7   Kerygma – Acts 2:22-36 –

8   No one can come to me unless the Father who sent me draws him (John

repents and turns from his sins,[1] is redeemed,[2] declared wholly righteous,[3] born again,[4] made alive in Christ as a new creature,[5] reconciled to God,[6] becomes a child of God,[7] and is

---

6:44).

1   Repentance – Repent and be baptized every one of you in the name of Jesus Christ for the forgiveness of your sins, and you will receive the gift of the Holy Spirit (Acts 2:38).

2   Redemption – And they sang a new song, saying, "Worthy are you to take the scroll and to open its seals, for you were slain, and by your blood you ransomed people for God from every tribe and language and people and nation" (Rev 5:9).

3   Justification – For I am not ashamed of the gospel, for it is the power of God for salvation to everyone who believes, to the Jew first and also to the Greek For in it the righteousness of God is revealed from faith for faith, as it is written, "The righteous shall live by faith" (Rom 1:16-17). But now the righteousness of God has been manifested apart from the law, although the Law and the Prophets bear witness to it—the righteousness of God through faith in Jesus Christ for all who believe. For there is no distinction: for all have sinned and fall short of the glory of God, and are justified by his grace as a gift, through the redemption that is in Christ Jesus, whom God put forward as a propitiation by his blood, to be received by faith. This was to show God's righteousness, because in his divine forbearance he had passed over former sins. It was to show his righteousness at the present time, so that he might be just and the justifier of the one who has faith in Jesus (Rom 3:21-26).

4   Regeneration – Jesus answered him, "Truly, truly, I say to you, unless one is born again he cannot see the kingdom of God.... Truly, truly, I say to you, unless one is born of water and the Spirit, he cannot enter the kingdom of God" (John 3:3, 5).

5   New creation – Therefore, if anyone is in Christ, he is a new creation. The old has passed away; behold, the new has come (2 Cor 5:17). Also Eph 4:20-24; Col 3:9.

6   Reconciliation – For if while we were enemies we were reconciled to God by the death of his Son, much more, now that we are reconciled, shall we be saved by his life (Rom 5:10).

7   Children of God – But to all who did receive him, who believed in his name, he gave the right to become children of God (John 1:12). See what kind of love the Father has given to us, that we should be called children of God; and so we are (1 John 3:1). The Spirit himself bears witness with our spirit that we are children of God, and if children, then heirs—heirs of God and fellow heirs with Christ, provided we suffer with him in order that we may also be glorified with him (Rom 8:16-17). See what kind of love the

filled with the fullness of the Holy Spirit[8] through whom he is empowered for a life of obedience.[9] The cross is sufficient to cover the sins of all who believe.[10] Ultimately, it is only the elect who believe.[11]

Father has given to us, that we should be called children of God; and so we are. The reason why the world does not know us is that it did not know him. Beloved, we are God's children now, and what we will be has not yet appeared; but we know that when he appears we shall be like him, because we shall see him as he is (1 John 3:1-2).

8   Holy Spirit – And Peter said to them, "Repent and be baptized every one of you in the name of Jesus Christ for the forgiveness of your sins, and you will receive the gift of the Holy Spirit" (Acts 2:38). For all who are led by the Spirit of God are sons of God.... The Spirit himself bears witness with our spirit that we are children of God, and if children, then heirs—heirs of God and fellow heirs with Christ, provided we suffer with him in order that we may also be glorified with him (Rom 8:14,16-17).

9   Sanctification – see Article Seven: Sanctification.

10   Sufficiency – If, because of one man's trespass, death reigned through that one man, much more will those who receive the abundance of grace and the free gift of righteousness reign in life through the one man Jesus Christ. Therefore, as one trespass led to condemnation for all men, so one act of righteousness leads to justification and life for all men. For as by the one man's disobedience the many were made sinners, so by the one man's obedience the many will be made righteous (Rom 5:17-19).

11   Election – Rom 9:6-29 – For those whom he foreknew he also predestined to be conformed to the image of his Son, in order that he might be the firstborn among many brothers. And those whom he predestined he also called, and those whom he called he also justified, and those whom he justified he also glorified (Rom 8:29-30). He chose us in him before the foundation of the world (Eph 1:4). All who dwell on earth will worship it, everyone whose name has not been written before the foundation of the world in the book of life of the Lamb that was slain (Rev 13:8). You do not believe because you are not part of my flock. My sheep hear my voice, and I know them, and they follow me. I give them eternal life, and they will never perish, and no one will snatch them out of my hand. My Father, who has given them to me, is greater than all, and no one is able to snatch them out of the Father's hand (John 10:26-29). As many as were appointed to eternal life believed (Acts 13:48).

VIII. ARTICLE EIGHT: SANCTIFICATION (DOCTRINE OF HOLINESS)

God's will for every believer is his sanctification.[1] It is the necessary[2] and certain[3] fruit of salvation, yet not meritorious; it is God alone who saves.[4] Through the work of the Spirit, saints are called and enabled to live lives of holiness,[5] "in" but not "of" the world,[6] fully dedicated disciples of Jesus

---

[1] Rom 6 – For this is the will of God, your sanctification (1 Thess 4:3). What shall we say then? Are we to continue in sin that grace may abound? By no means! How can we who died to sin still live in it? (Rom 6:1-2). What then? Are we to sin because we are not under law but under grace? By no means! Do you not know that if you present yourselves to anyone as obedient slaves, you are slaves of the one whom you obey, either of sin, which leads to death, or of obedience, which leads to righteousness? (Rom 6:15-16).

[2] Necessity – Rom 6, Jas 1:19-25; 2:14-26; – Whoever says "I know him" but does not keep his commandments is a liar, and the truth is not in him, but whoever keeps his word, in him truly the love of God is perfected. By this we may be sure that we are in him: whoever says he abides in him ought to walk in the same way in which he walked (1 John 2:4-6). Strive for peace with everyone, and for the holiness without which no one will see the Lord (Heb 12:14).

[3] Transformation –

[4] See Article Six.

[5] Therefore, my beloved, as you have always obeyed, so now, not only as in my presence but much more in my absence, work out your own salvation with fear and trembling, for it is God who works in you, both to will and to work for his good pleasure (Phil 2:12-13). For this I toil, struggling with all his energy that he powerfully works within me (Col 1:29). Now may the God of peace who brought again from the dead our Lord Jesus, the great shepherd of the sheep, by the blood of the eternal covenant, equip you with everything good that you may do his will, working in us that which is pleasing in his sight, through Jesus Christ, to whom be glory forever and ever. Amen (Heb 13:20-21).

[6] I do not ask that you take them out of the world, but that you keep them from the evil one. They are not of the world, just as I am not of the world (John 17:15-16).

Christ,[7] persevering to the end.[8] Disciples are declared to be sanctified through the work of Christ[9] and are also called to become sanctified in the experiences of life.[10] The disciple's life will be characterized, among many,[11] by battle with sin,[12]

---

7   Lordship – Mark 8:34-38; 9:33-37; Matt 5:8; 6:19-24 – Go therefore and make disciples of all nations, baptizing them in the name of the Father and of the Son and of the Holy Spirit, teaching them to observe all that I have commanded you. And behold, I am with you always, to the end of the age (Matt 28:19-20).

8   Perseverance – warning passages in Hebrews (3-4; 5:11-6:20; 10:26-31) – But the one who endures to the end will be saved (Matt 24:13). For we share in Christ, if indeed we hold our original confidence firm to the end (Heb 3:14). And you, who once were alienated and hostile in mind, doing evil deeds, he has now reconciled in his body of flesh by his death, in order to present you holy and blameless and above reproach before him, if indeed you continue in the faith, stable and steadfast, not shifting from the hope of the gospel that you heard, which has been proclaimed in all creation under heaven, and of which I, Paul, became a minister (Col 1:21-23). The Spirit himself bears witness with our spirit that we are children of God, and if children, then heirs – heirs of God and fellow heirs with Christ, provided we suffer with him in order that we may also be glorified with him (Rom 8:16-17). And I saw the dead, great and small, standing before the throne, and books were opened. Then another book was opened, which is the book of life. And the dead were judged by what was written in the books, according to what they had done (Rev 20:12). They went out from us, but they were not of us; for if they had been of us, they would have continued with us. But they went out, that it might become plain that they all are not of us (1 John 2:19). Do not fear what you are about to suffer. Behold, the devil is about to throw some of you into prison, that you may be tested, and for ten days you will have tribulation. Be faithful unto death, and I will give you the crown of life. He who has an ear, let him hear what the Spirit says to the churches. The one who conquers will not be hurt by the second death.... The one who conquers will be clothed thus in white garments, and I will never blot his name out of the book of life. I will confess his name before my Father and before his angels (Rev 2:10-11; 3:5). Also discussion of the Holy Spirit as our guarantor.

9   Positional sanctification –

10 Experiential sanctification –

11 Rom 12; Gal 5:16-6:10; Eph 4-6; Phil 4:4-9; Col 3; 1 Thess 4:1-12; 5:14-22.

12 1 John 1:5-2:6; Rom 7 –

repentance,[1] sexual purity,[2] gracious speech,[3] prayer,[4]

---

1 Repentance – If we say we have fellowship with him while we walk in darkness, we lie and do not practice the truth. But if we walk in the light, as he is in the light, we have fellowship with one another, and the blood of Jesus his Son cleanses us from all sin. If we say we have no sin, we deceive ourselves, and the truth is not in us. If we confess our sins, he is faithful and just to forgive us our sins and to cleanse us from all unrighteousness (1 John 1:6-9).

2 Finally, then, brothers, we ask and urge you in the Lord Jesus, that as you received from us how you ought to live and to please God, just as you are doing, that you do so more and more. For you know what instructions we gave you through the Lord Jesus. For this is the will of God, your sanctification: that you abstain from sexual immorality; that each one of you know how to control his own body in holiness and honor, not in the passion of lust like the Gentiles who do not know God; that no one transgress and wrong his brother in this matter, because the Lord is an avenger in all these things, as we told you beforehand and solemnly warned you. For God has not called us for impurity, but in holiness. Therefore whoever disregards this, disregards not man but God, who gives his Holy Spirit to you (1 Thess 4:1-8). But sexual immorality and all impurity or covetousness must not even be named among you, as is proper among saints. For you may be sure of this, that everyone who is sexually immoral or impure, or who is covetous (that is, an idolater), has no inheritance in the kingdom of Christ and God (Eph 5:3,5). Do not be unequally yoked with unbelievers. For what partnership has righteousness with lawlessness? Or what fellowship has light with darkness? What accord has Christ with Belial? Or what portion does a believer share with an unbeliever? What agreement has the temple of God with idols? For we are the temple of the living God; as God said, "I will make my dwelling among them and walk among them, and I will be their God, and they shall be my people. Therefore go out from their midst, and be separate from them, says the Lord, and touch no unclean thing; then I will welcome you, and I will be a father to you, and you shall be sons and daughters to me, says the Lord Almighty" (2 Cor 6:14-18).

3 Tongue – James 3:1-12 – Let no corrupting talk come out of your mouths, but only such as is good for building up, as fits the occasion, that it may give grace to those who hear (Eph 4:29). Let there be no filthiness nor foolish talk nor crude joking, which are out of place, but instead let there be thanksgiving (Eph 5:4). Do all things without grumbling or questioning (Phil 2:14). If anyone thinks he is religious and does not bridle his tongue but deceives his heart, this person's religion is worthless (Jas 1:26).

4 Matt 6:7-15; James 5:13-20 –

suffering,[5] persecution,[6] being different from the world,[7] living

---

5   Suffering — Through him we have also obtained access by faith into this grace in which we stand, and we rejoice in hope of the glory of God. More than that, we rejoice in our sufferings, knowing that suffering produces endurance, and endurance produces character, and character produces hope, and hope does not put us to shame, because God's love has been poured into our hearts through the Holy Spirit who has been given to us (Rom 5:2-5). In this you rejoice, though now for a little while, if necessary, you have been grieved by various trials, so that the tested genuineness of your faith—more precious than gold that perishes though it is tested by fire—may be found to result in praise and glory and honor at the revelation of Jesus Christ (1 Pet 1:6-7). But even if you should suffer for righteousness' sake, you will be blessed (1 Pet 3:14). But rejoice insofar as you share Christ's sufferings, that you may also rejoice and be glad when his glory is revealed (1 Pet 4:13). Yet if anyone suffers as a Christian, let him not be ashamed, but let him glorify God in that name (1 Pet 4:16). And we know that for those who love God all things work together for good, for those who are called according to his purpose. For those whom he foreknew he also predestined to be conformed to the image of his Son, in order that he might be the firstborn among many brothers (Rom 8:28-29). For I consider that the sufferings of this present time are not worth comparing with the glory that is to be revealed to us (Rom 8:18). Count it all joy, my brothers, when you meet trials of various kinds, for you know that the testing of your faith produces steadfastness. And let steadfastness have its full effect, that you may be perfect and complete, lacking in nothing (Jas 1:2-4).

6   Persecution — Blessed are those who are persecuted for righteousness' sake, for theirs is the kingdom of heaven. Blessed are you when others revile you and persecute you and utter all kinds of evil against you falsely on my account. Rejoice and be glad, for your reward is great in heaven, for so they persecuted the prophets who were before you (Matt 5:10-12). Indeed, all who desire to live a godly life in Christ Jesus will be persecuted (2 Tim 3:12). Also Heb 12:3-17.

7   Different — You are the salt of the earth, but if salt has lost its taste, how shall its saltiness be restored? It is no longer good for anything except to be thrown out and trampled under people's feet. You are the light of the world. A city set on a hill cannot be hidden. Nor do people light a lamp and put it under a basket, but on a stand, and it gives light to all in the house. In the same way, let your light shine before others, so that they may see your good works and give glory to your Father who is in heaven (Matt 5:13-16). I appeal to you therefore, brothers, by the mercies of God, to present your bodies as a living sacrifice, holy and acceptable to God, which is your spiritual worship. Do not be conformed to this world, but be transformed by the renewal of your mind, that by testing you may discern what is the will of God, what is good and acceptable and perfect (Rom 12:1-2). Therefore go out from their midst, and be separate from them, says the Lord (2 Cor 6:17). For they

for the glory of God.[1] Growth toward holiness brings with it assurance of salvation[2] and a desire to share the gospel with sinners.[3]

---

themselves report concerning us the kind of reception we had among you, and how you turned to God from idols to serve the living and true God, and to wait for his Son from heaven, whom he raised from the dead, Jesus who delivers us from the wrath to come (1 Thess 9-10).

1   So, whether you eat or drink, or whatever you do, do all to the glory of God (1 Cor 10:31). What if God, desiring to show his wrath and to make known his power, has endured with much patience vessels of wrath prepared for destruction, in order to make known the riches of his glory for vessels of mercy, which he has prepared beforehand for glory (Rom 9:22-23).

2   Assurance – My little children, I am writing these things to you so that you may not sin. But if anyone does sin, we have an advocate with the Father, Jesus Christ the righteous. He is the propitiation for our sins, and not for ours only but also for the sins of the whole world. And by this we know that we have come to know him, if we keep his commandments. Whoever says "I know him" but does not keep his commandments is a liar, and the truth is not in him, but whoever keeps his word, in him truly the love of God is perfected. By this we may be sure that we are in him: whoever says he abides in him ought to walk in the same way in which he walked (1 John 2:1-6). By this it is evident who are the children of God, and who are the children of the devil: whoever does not practice righteousness is not of God, nor is the one who does not love his brother (1 John 3:10). We know that we have passed out of death into life, because we love the brothers. Whoever does not love abides in death (1 John 3:14). Whoever keeps his commandments abides in him, and he in them. And by this we know that he abides in us, by the Spirit whom he has given us (1 John 3:24). And we have seen and testify that the Father has sent his Son to be the Savior of the world (1 John 4:14). The Spirit himself bears witness with our spirit that we are children of God, and if children, then heirs—heirs of God and fellow heirs with Christ, provided we suffer with him in order that we may also be glorified with him (Rom 8:16-17). Consequently, he is able to save to the uttermost those who draw near to God through him, since he always lives to make intercession for them (Heb 7:25). Therefore, brothers, since we have confidence to enter the holy places by the blood of Jesus, by the new and living way that he opened for us through the curtain, that is, through his flesh, and since we have a great priest over the house of God, let us draw near with a true heart in full assurance of faith, with our hearts sprinkled clean from an evil conscience and our bodies washed with pure water (Heb 10:19-22). Also Rom 9:15-24.

3   Evangelism – In your hearts regard Christ the Lord as holy, always being prepared to make a defense to anyone who asks you for a reason for the hope that is in you (1 Pet 3:15).

IX. ARTICLE NINE: ECCLESIOLOGY (DOCTRINE OF THE CHURCH)

The church consists of all true disciples of Jesus Christ.[4] All things exist under the supremacy of Christ, and therefore Christ and Christ alone is the head of the church.[5] The local expression of the church is comprised of disciples gifted for the work of building up the body of Christ,[6] living in unity,[7] bound together by love.[8] While different local expressions may have different emphases, all are commanded to make disciples, which includes both evangelism and teaching obedience to all that Jesus taught.[9] The church is to be committed to the reading of Scripture, the exhortation to

---

4   Body of Christ –

5   Headship of Christ – And he put all things under his feet and gave him as head over all things to the church, which is his body, the fullness of him who fills all in all (Eph 1:22-23). Go therefore and make disciples of all nations, baptizing them in the name of the Father and of the Son and of the Holy Spirit, teaching them to observe all that I have commanded you. And behold, I am with you always, to the end of the age (Matt 28:19-20).

6   Spiritual gifts – To each is given the manifestation of the Spirit for the common good (1 Cor 12:7).

7   Unity – I do not ask for these only, but also for those who will believe in me through their word, that they may all be one, just as you, Father, are in me, and I in you, that they also may be in us, so that the world may believe that you have sent me. The glory that you have given me I have given to them, that they may be one even as we are one, I in them and you in me, that they may become perfectly one, so that the world may know that you sent me and loved them even as you loved me. Father, I desire that they also, whom you have given me, may be with me where I am, to see my glory that you have given me because you loved me before the foundation of the world. O righteous Father, even though the world does not know you, I know you, and these know that you have sent me. I made known to them your name, and I will continue to make it known, that the love with which you have loved me may be in them, and I in them (John 17:20-26). Also Phil 1:27-2:11

8   Love – 1 John 2:7-17.

9   Balance – Go therefore and make disciples of all nations, baptizing them in the name of the Father and of the Son and of the Holy Spirit, teaching them to observe all that I have commanded you. And behold, I am with you always, to the end of the age (Matt 28:19-20).

obedience, and teaching of the doctrinal truths of Scripture,[1] as well as to all that is necessary for the edification of the body, including worship, singing, prayer, and service, all to the glory of God.[2]

Baptism and the Lord's Supper are ordinances to be valued and observed.[3] They are visible signs representing spiritual truths; they do not accomplish salvation.[4] Baptism is the washing of the believer, signifying that in conversion he has died to his old life and has been raised with Christ into a newness of life in which the power of sin is broken.[5] The Lord's Supper is the present proclamation of Christ's atoning death, and looks forward to his return.[6]

---

[1] Worship – Devote yourself to the public reading of Scripture, to exhortation, to teaching (1 Tim 4:13).

[2] Worship – Addressing one another in psalms and hymns and spiritual songs, singing and making melody to the Lord with all your heart (Eph 5:19). Let the word of Christ dwell in you richly, teaching and admonishing one another in all wisdom, singing psalms and hymns and spiritual songs, with thankfulness in your hearts to God (Col 3:16). So, whether you eat or drink, or whatever you do, do all to the glory of God (1 Cor 10:31).

[3] Valued – And Jesus came and said to them, "All authority in heaven and on earth has been given to me. Go therefore and make disciples of all nations, baptizing them in the name of the Father and of the Son and of the Holy Spirit, teaching them to observe all that I have commanded you. And behold, I am with you always, to the end of the age" (Matt 28:18-20). And Peter said to them, "Repent and be baptized every one of you in the name of Jesus Christ for the forgiveness of your sins, and you will receive the gift of the Holy Spirit" (Acts 2:38).

[4] Baptism, which corresponds to this, now saves you, not as a removal of dirt from the body but as an appeal to God for a good conscience, through the resurrection of Jesus Christ (1 Pet 3:21).

[5] Baptism – Do you not know that all of us who have been baptized into Christ Jesus were baptized into his death? We were buried therefore with him by baptism into death, in order that, just as Christ was raised from the dead by the glory of the Father, we too might walk in newness of life (Rom 6:3-4). Baptism, which corresponds to this, now saves you, not as a removal of dirt from the body but as an appeal to God for a good conscience, through the resurrection of Jesus Christ (1 Pet 3:21).

[6] Lord's Supper – Mark 14:12-25; 1 Cor 11:17-34 – For as often as you eat this bread and drink the cup, you proclaim the Lord's death until he

X. ARTICLE TEN: ESCHATOLOGY (DOCTRINE OF LAST THINGS)

Jesus will return—personally, visibly to all, suddenly[7]—and all disciples living and dead will be bodily caught up to meet Him.[8] At the final judgment, the unrepentant will be raised to the resurrection of judgment and everlasting punishment in hell.[9] Believers, while already having passed from darkness to light,[10] will be raised[11] to the resurrection of life,[12] and will enjoy the everlasting, personal presence of God in His heavenly kingdom.[13] God's plan of creation, redemption, and

---

comes (1 Cor 11:26).

7   Return – Mark 13; Matt 24-25; 1 Thess 4:13-5:11; 2 Thess 2:1-12; Revelation –

8   Rapture – For the Lord himself will descend from heaven with a cry of command, with the voice of an archangel, and with the sound of the trumpet of God. And the dead in Christ will rise first. Then we who are alive, who are left, will be caught up together with them in the clouds to meet the Lord in the air, and so we will always be with the Lord (1 Thess 4:16-17).

9   Final judgment of Wicked – Then I saw a great white throne and him who was seated on it. From his presence earth and sky fled away, and no place was found for them. And I saw the dead, great and small, standing before the throne, and books were opened. Then another book was opened, which is the book of life. And the dead were judged by what was written in the books, according to what they had done. And the sea gave up the dead who were in it, Death and Hades gave up the dead who were in them, and they were judged, each one of them, according to what they had done. Then Death and Hades were thrown into the lake of fire. This is the second death, the lake of fire. And if anyone's name was not found written in the book of life, he was thrown into the lake of fire (Rev 20:11-15).

10   Realized eschatology –

11   Resurrection – 1 Cor 15; 2 Cor 5:1-10 –

12   Rev 19-22 –

13   Final judgment of Righteous – And I heard a loud voice from the throne saying, "Behold, the dwelling place of God is with man. He will dwell with them, and they will be his people, and God himself will be with them as their God. He will wipe away every tear from their eyes, and death shall be no more, neither shall there be mourning nor crying nor pain anymore, for the former things have passed away" (Rev 21:3-4).

glorification will be complete.[1]

This is the hope for which we long, which helps to motivate us now toward godly living, and which propels us to share the gospel of Jesus Christ with a lost and dying world.

---

[1] And those whom he predestined he also called, and those whom he called he also justified, and those whom he justified he also glorified (Rom 8:30).

Made in the USA
Coppell, TX
14 February 2023